GITHUB COPILOT

FOR DEVELOPERS

SMART CODING WITH AI PAIR PROGRAMMER

4 BOOKS IN 1

BOOK 1
GITHUB COPILOT COMPANION: AN INTRODUCTION TO AI-ASSISTED PROGRAMMING

BOOK 2
MASTERING AI PAIR PROGRAMMING: ADVANCED TECHNIQUES FOR DEVELOPERS

BOOK 3
EFFICIENT CODING WITH GITHUB COPILOT: STRATEGIES FOR INTERMEDIATE DEVELOPERS

BOOK 4
EXPERT INSIGHTS: LEVERAGING GITHUB COPILOT FOR COMPLEX DEVELOPMENT TASKS

ROB BOTWRIGHT

Published by Rob Botwright
Library of Congress Cataloging-in-Publication Data
ISBN 978-1-83938-755-5
Cover design by Rizzo

Disclaimer

The contents of this book are based on extensive research and the best available historical sources. However, the author and publisher make no claims, promises, or guarantees about the accuracy, completeness, or adequacy of the information contained herein. The information in this book is provided on an "as is" basis, and the author and publisher disclaim any and all liability for any errors, omissions, or inaccuracies in the information or for any actions taken in reliance on such information. The opinions and views expressed in this book are those of the author and do not necessarily reflect the official policy or position of any organization or individual mentioned in this book. Any reference to specific people, places, or events is intended only to provide historical context and is not intended to defame or malign any group, individual, or entity. The information in this book is intended for educational and entertainment purposes only. It is not intended to be a substitute for professional advice or judgment. Readers are encouraged to conduct their own research and to seek professional advice where appropriate. Every effort has been made to obtain necessary permissions and acknowledgments for all images and other copyrighted material used in this book. Any errors or omissions in this regard are unintentional, and the author and publisher will correct them in future editions.

BOOK 1 - GITHUB COPILOT COMPANION: AN INTRODUCTION TO AI-ASSISTED PROGRAMMING

BOOK 2 - MASTERING AI PAIR PROGRAMMING: ADVANCED TECHNIQUES FOR DEVELOPERS

BOOK 3 - EFFICIENT CODING WITH GITHUB COPILOT: STRATEGIES FOR INTERMEDIATE DEVELOPERS

BOOK 4 - EXPERT INSIGHTS: LEVERAGING GITHUB COPILOT FOR COMPLEX DEVELOPMENT TASKS

Introduction

Welcome to "GitHub Copilot for Developers: Smart Coding with AI Pair Programmer," a comprehensive book bundle designed to empower developers with the knowledge and skills needed to harness the power of AI-assisted programming using GitHub Copilot. In this bundle, consisting of four distinct volumes, readers will embark on a journey from introductory concepts to advanced techniques, exploring how Copilot can revolutionize their development workflows and enhance their coding proficiency.

Book 1: "GitHub Copilot Companion: An Introduction to AI-Assisted Programming," serves as the foundation for understanding the fundamentals of AI-assisted programming and introduces readers to the capabilities of GitHub Copilot. Through practical examples and guided exercises, readers will learn how Copilot generates contextually relevant code suggestions, accelerating the coding process and reducing development time.

Building upon the foundation laid in Book 1, Book 2: "Mastering AI Pair Programming: Advanced Techniques for Developers," delves deeper into the intricacies of AI pair programming. Here, readers will explore advanced techniques and strategies for maximizing productivity and efficiency with Copilot. From optimizing code generation to integrating Copilot seamlessly into existing workflows, developers will gain the skills needed to tackle complex coding challenges with confidence.

Book 3: "Efficient Coding with GitHub Copilot: Strategies for Intermediate Developers," caters to the needs of intermediate developers seeking to refine their coding skills and streamline their development processes. Through a series of best practices and optimization strategies, readers will learn how to leverage Copilot to write cleaner, more maintainable code and enhance their overall coding efficiency.

Finally, in Book 4: "Expert Insights: Leveraging GitHub Copilot for Complex Development Tasks," readers will gain access to expert insights and real-world use cases showcasing the full potential of Copilot in addressing complex development tasks. From refactoring legacy codebases to scaling Copilot usage for large-scale projects, developers will learn how to harness Copilot's AI capabilities to overcome challenges and drive innovation in their projects.

Whether you are a beginner exploring the possibilities of AI-assisted programming or a seasoned professional seeking to optimize your development workflow, "GitHub Copilot for Developers" provides a comprehensive guide to unlocking the full potential of Copilot. With AI as your trusted pair programmer, you can embark on your coding journey with confidence, efficiency, and creativity, paving the way for a future of smarter, more collaborative software development.

BOOK 1
GITHUB COPILOT COMPANION
AN INTRODUCTION TO AI-ASSISTED PROGRAMMING

ROB BOTWRIGHT

Chapter 1: Introduction to GitHub Copilot

GitHub Copilot revolutionizes the landscape of software development, seamlessly integrating artificial intelligence (AI) into the coding process. With Copilot, developers are empowered with an advanced tool that assists in generating code snippets, offering suggestions, and enhancing productivity. Harnessing the power of OpenAI's GPT-3 model, Copilot brings unprecedented capabilities to programmers, enabling them to tackle complex coding challenges with ease. Leveraging machine learning algorithms, Copilot analyzes code contexts and offers intelligent suggestions, significantly streamlining the development workflow.

One of the key features of GitHub Copilot is its ability to provide context-aware code completions, drastically reducing the time and effort required for coding tasks. By analyzing the codebase and understanding the developer's intent, Copilot suggests relevant code snippets in real-time, allowing developers to focus on solving higher-level problems rather than getting bogged down in mundane coding details. This feature is particularly beneficial for beginners, as it helps them learn coding patterns and best practices by providing instant feedback and guidance.

Moreover, GitHub Copilot excels in assisting developers with writing boilerplate code, eliminating the need for manual typing of repetitive code segments. Whether it's initializing variables, defining classes, or handling common programming constructs, Copilot suggests concise and accurate code snippets, saving valuable development time. Developers can leverage Copilot's suggestions to quickly scaffold project structures, prototypes, and code frameworks, jumpstarting their development process.

In addition to code completions, GitHub Copilot offers advanced refactoring capabilities, enabling developers to improve code quality and maintainability effortlessly. By analyzing existing code snippets and identifying potential optimizations, Copilot suggests refactorings that adhere to industry best practices and coding standards. Whether it's renaming variables, extracting methods, or optimizing algorithms, Copilot provides intelligent suggestions that help streamline code maintenance and enhance overall codebase quality.

Another notable aspect of GitHub Copilot is its collaborative features, which facilitate team-based development and knowledge sharing. With Copilot, developers can collaborate in real-time, leveraging its suggestions and insights to iterate on code together. This fosters a collaborative coding environment where team members can leverage each other's expertise and collectively solve complex programming challenges. Moreover, Copilot's integration with version control systems like Git enables seamless collaboration and code review workflows, ensuring code consistency and quality across the development lifecycle.

Furthermore, GitHub Copilot is highly customizable, allowing developers to tailor its behavior and preferences to suit their individual workflow. From adjusting code generation preferences to defining custom code templates, developers have full control over how Copilot assists them in their coding tasks. This flexibility enables developers to adapt Copilot to their specific programming style and project requirements, maximizing its utility and effectiveness.

Deploying GitHub Copilot is straightforward, requiring only a few simple steps to integrate it into the development environment. After installing the Copilot extension for supported code editors such as Visual Studio Code, developers can activate it within their coding sessions. Once activated, Copilot analyzes the code context and provides suggestions in real-time, enhancing the coding experience and productivity. Additionally, developers can fine-tune Copilot's behavior and preferences through the extension settings, ensuring optimal integration with their workflow.

In summary, GitHub Copilot represents a paradigm shift in software development, empowering developers with AI-assisted coding capabilities that enhance productivity, code quality, and collaboration. By leveraging machine learning algorithms and context-aware code analysis, Copilot provides intelligent suggestions and automations that streamline the coding process. With its customizable features and seamless integration into existing development workflows, Copilot is poised to become an indispensable tool for developers across various industries and skill levels, shaping the future of software development.

The history of artificial intelligence (AI) in programming traces back to the early days of computing, where pioneers envisioned machines capable of reasoning and problem-solving akin to human intelligence. One of the earliest manifestations of AI in programming dates back to the mid-20th century, with the development of symbolic AI systems such as the Logic Theorist by Allen Newell and Herbert A. Simon in 1956. This groundbreaking system demonstrated the potential of AI to automate logical reasoning tasks, laying the foundation for subsequent developments in the field.

As computing technology advanced, so did the aspirations of AI researchers to create intelligent software agents capable of performing increasingly complex tasks. In the 1960s and 1970s, researchers explored various approaches to AI, including expert systems, rule-based programming, and natural language processing. These efforts led to the development of early AI programming languages and frameworks, such as LISP and Prolog, which enabled developers to implement AI algorithms and applications.

Throughout the 1980s and 1990s, AI in programming experienced both periods of optimism and disillusionment, often referred to as AI summers and winters, respectively. Despite setbacks and challenges, researchers continued to make significant strides in AI technology, leading to the emergence of new paradigms such as neural networks and machine learning. These advancements paved the way for breakthroughs in AI programming, including the development of intelligent agents, pattern recognition systems, and autonomous decision-making algorithms.

In the early 21st century, the convergence of AI and programming reached new heights with the advent of deep learning and data-driven approaches to AI. Enabled by the proliferation of big data and advancements in computational hardware, deep learning algorithms revolutionized various domains, including natural language processing, computer vision, and speech recognition. These advances fueled the development of AI-powered programming tools and platforms, ushering in a new era of AI-assisted programming.

One of the most notable developments in recent years is the rise of AI programming assistants, such as GitHub Copilot, which leverage machine learning models to assist developers in writing code. GitHub Copilot, powered by OpenAI's GPT-3 model, analyzes code contexts and generates intelligent code completions and suggestions in real-time. This innovative tool represents a significant milestone in the evolution of AI in programming, democratizing access to AI-assisted coding capabilities and empowering developers to write code more efficiently and effectively.

Deploying GitHub Copilot is straightforward, requiring developers to install the Copilot extension for their preferred code editor, such as Visual Studio Code. Once installed, developers can activate Copilot within their coding sessions, allowing it to provide context-aware code suggestions and completions. By seamlessly integrating AI into the programming workflow, Copilot enables developers to focus on solving higher-level problems while automating repetitive coding tasks.

Looking ahead, the future of AI in programming holds immense promise, with ongoing research and development efforts focused on advancing AI capabilities and applications in software development. From enhancing code quality and productivity to enabling new forms of human-machine collaboration, AI continues to reshape the way developers write and maintain software. As AI technologies continue to evolve and mature, they will undoubtedly play an increasingly integral role in shaping the future of programming and software development.

Chapter 2: Understanding AI-Assisted Programming

AI-assisted programming has emerged as a transformative approach to software development, leveraging artificial intelligence (AI) to augment the capabilities of developers and streamline the coding process. At its core, AI-assisted programming embodies several key principles that underpin its effectiveness and utility in modern software development workflows. One fundamental principle is the integration of AI into the development environment, enabling developers to leverage AI-powered tools and services seamlessly. This integration is often facilitated through code editors and integrated development environments (IDEs) that support AI-assisted features, such as code completion, refactoring suggestions, and error detection.

One of the foundational principles of AI-assisted programming is the emphasis on context-awareness, wherein AI algorithms analyze the code context and developer's intent to provide relevant suggestions and insights. This context-awareness enables AI-assisted tools to understand the semantics of the code being written and offer intelligent recommendations that align with the developer's goals. For example, AI-powered code completion systems like GitHub Copilot analyze the codebase, comments, and variable names to generate contextually relevant code snippets in real-time. By understanding the context in which code is written, AI-assisted programming tools enhance developer productivity and code quality.

Another principle of AI-assisted programming is the provision of actionable insights and suggestions that aid developers in solving coding challenges more effectively. AI-powered programming assistants leverage machine learning algorithms to analyze large datasets of code examples and patterns, enabling them to identify common coding pitfalls, suggest best practices, and offer alternative solutions. For instance, tools like DeepCode analyze code repositories to detect potential bugs, security vulnerabilities, and code smells, providing developers with actionable recommendations to improve code quality.

Furthermore, AI-assisted programming embraces the principle of adaptability, wherein AI algorithms continuously learn and adapt to developers' coding styles, preferences, and feedback. This adaptability enables AI-powered tools to evolve over time and become more personalized and effective in assisting developers. For example, AI-based code completion systems can learn from developers' code edits and preferences to refine their suggestions and predictions, improving their accuracy and relevance. By adapting to developers' individual needs and workflows, AI-assisted programming tools become indispensable companions in the software development process.

Moreover, AI-assisted programming emphasizes the importance of transparency and explainability, enabling developers to understand how AI algorithms make recommendations and decisions. Transparency ensures that developers have visibility into the inner workings of AI-assisted tools, allowing them to trust and validate the suggestions provided. Explainability, on the other hand, enables AI-powered systems to provide rationale and justification for their recommendations, helping developers understand the reasoning behind the suggested code changes. By fostering transparency and explainability, AI-assisted programming tools empower developers to make informed decisions and collaborate effectively with AI algorithms.

Deploying AI-assisted programming techniques often involves integrating AI-powered tools and services into existing development workflows. For example, to leverage GitHub Copilot, developers can install the Copilot extension for their preferred code editor, such as Visual Studio Code, and activate it within their coding sessions. Similarly, tools like DeepCode can be integrated into code repositories and continuous integration pipelines to automatically analyze code changes and provide feedback to developers. By seamlessly integrating AI-assisted programming tools into their workflows, developers can harness the power of AI to enhance their productivity and code quality.

In summary, the principles of AI-assisted programming embody the core tenets that guide the development and deployment of AI-powered tools and services in software development. By integrating AI into the development environment, emphasizing context-awareness, providing actionable insights, fostering adaptability, and prioritizing transparency and explainability, AI-assisted programming tools empower developers to write better code more efficiently. As AI technologies continue to evolve and mature, they will undoubtedly play an increasingly integral role in shaping the future of programming and software development.

GitHub Copilot, a groundbreaking tool developed by GitHub in collaboration with OpenAI, harnesses state-of-the-art artificial intelligence (AI) models and algorithms to provide intelligent code suggestions and completions to developers. At the heart of Copilot lies OpenAI's GPT (Generative Pre-trained Transformer) model, specifically GPT-3, which powers its language understanding and generation capabilities. GPT-3, renowned for its ability to generate human-like text based on input prompts, forms the backbone of Copilot's AI-driven code generation functionality. This powerful model, trained on vast amounts of text data from the internet, has been fine-tuned specifically for code-related tasks, enabling Copilot to understand and generate code snippets across various programming languages and domains.

Deploying GitHub Copilot typically involves installing the Copilot extension for supported code editors, such as Visual Studio Code, and activating it within the coding environment. Once activated, Copilot integrates seamlessly into the developer's workflow, analyzing code contexts and providing intelligent suggestions and completions in real-time. Under the hood, Copilot leverages GPT-3's language understanding capabilities to parse and interpret the code being written, enabling it to generate contextually relevant code snippets based on the developer's input.

In addition to GPT-3, GitHub Copilot incorporates a range of AI algorithms and techniques to enhance its code generation and suggestion capabilities. These include recurrent neural networks (RNNs), which are commonly used in natural language processing tasks, and transformer architectures, such as the Transformer model underlying GPT-3, which excel at capturing long-range dependencies in sequential data. By leveraging a combination of these AI algorithms, Copilot is able to analyze code contexts, understand programming patterns, and generate syntactically correct and semantically meaningful code snippets.

Furthermore, GitHub Copilot incorporates advanced techniques for code completion and suggestion, such as code tokenization and semantic parsing, to enhance the accuracy and relevance of its suggestions. Tokenization involves breaking down code into smaller units, or tokens, which are then fed into the AI model for analysis and generation. Semantic parsing, on the other hand, involves extracting the meaning or semantics of code constructs, such as function calls and variable assignments, to generate contextually relevant suggestions. By combining tokenization and semantic parsing techniques, Copilot is able to generate precise and contextually appropriate code completions tailored to the developer's needs.

Another key aspect of Copilot's AI models and algorithms is their ability to adapt and learn from developer interactions over time. GitHub Copilot continuously refines its AI models based on feedback from developers, learning from the code edits and corrections made by users to improve the quality and relevance of its suggestions. This adaptive learning process enables Copilot to evolve and become more effective at assisting developers with their coding tasks over time, ultimately enhancing developer productivity and code quality.

Moreover, GitHub Copilot incorporates techniques for code synthesis and generation, enabling it to generate novel code snippets based on the patterns and examples it has learned from training data. This capability allows Copilot to assist developers in solving a wide range of coding tasks, from implementing common programming constructs to addressing more complex challenges. By synthesizing code based on its understanding of programming principles and patterns, Copilot provides developers with valuable insights and accelerates the coding process.

In summary, GitHub Copilot leverages a sophisticated array of AI models and algorithms, including GPT-3, recurrent neural networks, and transformer architectures, to provide intelligent code suggestions and completions to developers. Deployed as a code editor extension, Copilot seamlessly integrates into the developer's workflow, analyzing code contexts and generating contextually relevant code snippets in real-time. By continuously learning and adapting from developer interactions, Copilot evolves over time to become more effective at assisting developers with their coding tasks, ultimately enhancing productivity and code quality in software development workflows.

Chapter 3: Getting Started with GitHub Copilot

Setting up the GitHub Copilot environment is a crucial initial step for developers looking to leverage this powerful AI-assisted coding tool in their software development workflows. To begin, developers must ensure they have access to a supported code editor, such as Visual Studio Code, as Copilot operates primarily as an extension within these environments. The first step in setting up the Copilot environment involves installing the Copilot extension for the chosen code editor. This can typically be done through the editor's built-in extension marketplace or by downloading the extension package from the GitHub Copilot website and manually installing it via the editor's extension manager. Once the Copilot extension is installed, developers may need to sign in with their GitHub account credentials to activate the extension and access its features. This authentication step is necessary to ensure that Copilot can access the code repositories and other resources needed to provide intelligent code suggestions and completions. After signing in, developers may also have the option to customize their Copilot settings and preferences, such as enabling or disabling specific features or adjusting the AI model's behavior.

With the Copilot extension installed and configured, developers are now ready to start using Copilot within their coding sessions. To activate Copilot, developers can typically use a keyboard shortcut or access the extension directly from the editor's menu or toolbar.

Once activated, Copilot integrates seamlessly into the coding environment, analyzing the code context and providing intelligent suggestions and completions in real-time. Developers can interact with Copilot by typing code as they normally would, and Copilot will automatically generate relevant code suggestions based on the context and developer's input.

In addition to providing code suggestions and completions, GitHub Copilot also offers a range of other features and capabilities to enhance the coding experience. For example, Copilot can generate documentation comments, refactor code, and even assist with code navigation and exploration. These additional features further streamline the development process and help developers write better code more efficiently.

As developers continue to use Copilot in their coding sessions, they may encounter situations where they need to troubleshoot issues or adjust Copilot's behavior. GitHub provides comprehensive documentation and support resources for Copilot users, including guides, tutorials, and FAQs, to help address common questions and concerns. Developers can also reach out to the GitHub community for assistance or report any bugs or issues they encounter while using Copilot.

Moreover, GitHub Copilot is continuously evolving and receiving updates and improvements from GitHub and OpenAI. Developers can stay informed about the latest developments and updates to Copilot by following GitHub's official announcements and release notes. These updates may introduce new features, enhancements, and bug fixes to Copilot, ensuring that developers have access to the most up-to-date and reliable version of the tool.

In summary, setting up the GitHub Copilot environment is a straightforward process that involves installing the Copilot extension for a supported code editor, configuring the extension settings, and activating Copilot within the coding environment. Once set up, Copilot seamlessly integrates into the developer's workflow, providing intelligent code suggestions and completions to enhance productivity and code quality. By leveraging Copilot's features and capabilities, developers can write better code more efficiently and effectively, ultimately accelerating the software development process.

The journey of getting started with GitHub Copilot begins with the traditional "Hello World!" program, a timeless ritual in the realm of programming. This simple yet iconic program serves as the starting point for developers exploring new languages, frameworks, or tools, and GitHub Copilot is no exception. To begin, developers must first ensure they have access to a supported code editor, such as Visual Studio Code, where Copilot operates as an extension. Once the code editor is set up, developers can proceed to install the Copilot extension, either through the editor's built-in extension marketplace or by downloading the extension package from the GitHub Copilot website and manually installing it using the appropriate commands or graphical interface provided by the editor.

Once the Copilot extension is installed, developers can activate it within their coding environment, typically by using a keyboard shortcut or accessing the extension directly from the editor's menu or toolbar. With Copilot activated, developers are now ready to write their first lines of code with Copilot's assistance. In the case of the classic "Hello World!" program, developers can simply type the familiar print statement, followed by the string "Hello, World!", and let Copilot generate the rest of the code.

For example, in Python, developers can use the print() function to output the "Hello, World!" message to the console. With Copilot activated, developers can start typing the print() function, and Copilot will generate a completion suggestion that includes the necessary syntax and arguments for printing the desired message. Developers can then accept the suggestion and execute the code to see the "Hello, World!" message displayed in the console output.

In JavaScript, developers can achieve the same result using console.log() to output the "Hello, World!" message to the console. Again, with Copilot activated, developers can start typing console.log() and accept Copilot's completion suggestion to generate the code. Upon execution, the "Hello, World!" message will be logged to the console, confirming that Copilot is functioning correctly and assisting developers with their coding tasks.

Beyond the traditional "Hello, World!" program, GitHub Copilot can assist developers with a wide range of coding tasks and challenges across various programming languages and domains. Whether it's generating code snippets, suggesting refactorings, or providing documentation comments, Copilot's AI-driven capabilities can help developers write code more efficiently and effectively. As developers continue to use Copilot in their coding sessions, they will become more familiar with its features and capabilities, enabling them to leverage its assistance to tackle increasingly complex coding tasks.

In addition to its code generation capabilities, GitHub Copilot can also assist developers with code navigation and exploration. For example, developers can use Copilot to quickly jump to definitions, find references, or navigate through code files using keyboard shortcuts or commands provided by the editor. This functionality allows developers to navigate large codebases more efficiently and locate specific code snippets or functions with ease.

Furthermore, GitHub Copilot offers additional features and integrations to enhance the coding experience further. For example, Copilot can integrate with version control systems like Git, enabling developers to commit changes, create branches, and perform other version control operations directly from the code editor. Additionally, Copilot can integrate with code review tools and services, allowing developers to request reviews, provide feedback, and collaborate with teammates on code changes seamlessly.

As developers continue their journey with GitHub Copilot, they will discover new ways to leverage its AI-driven capabilities to streamline their development workflows and write better code more efficiently. Whether it's exploring advanced code generation techniques, optimizing code quality, or collaborating with teammates, Copilot empowers developers to unleash their creativity and productivity in the world of software development. With its intuitive interface, powerful features, and seamless integration into existing coding environments, Copilot is poised to become an indispensable companion for developers across various industries and skill levels.

Chapter 4: Exploring GitHub Copilot Features

In the realm of software development, code completion and suggestions play a pivotal role in enhancing productivity and efficiency for developers. These features, commonly found in modern code editors and integrated development environments (IDEs), provide intelligent assistance to developers by predicting and suggesting code snippets, keywords, and constructs based on the context of the code being written. Leveraging advanced algorithms and machine learning techniques, code completion and suggestion tools analyze code contexts, understand programming patterns, and offer relevant recommendations to assist developers in their coding tasks.

To begin utilizing code completion and suggestions, developers must first ensure they have access to a code editor or IDE that supports these features. Popular code editors such as Visual Studio Code, IntelliJ IDEA, and Sublime Text often come with built-in support for code completion and suggestions, making them accessible to a wide range of developers across different programming languages and platforms. Additionally, developers can customize the behavior and preferences of code completion and suggestion tools to align with their coding style and preferences, further enhancing their effectiveness and utility.

Once the code editor is set up, developers can start leveraging code completion and suggestions within their coding sessions. For example, when typing a variable name or method call, the code editor's code completion feature can suggest possible completions based on the characters typed so far, along with relevant documentation and information. Developers can then select the desired completion from the list provided by the code editor or continue typing to refine the suggestion further.

Moreover, code completion and suggestion tools can offer insights and recommendations beyond basic code completions. For instance, these tools can provide suggestions for fixing syntax errors, optimizing code performance, and adhering to coding standards and best practices. By analyzing the code context and identifying potential issues or improvements, code completion and suggestion tools empower developers to write cleaner, more efficient code and avoid common pitfalls and errors.

In addition to providing code completions and suggestions in real-time, code editors often offer features for enhancing the accuracy and relevance of suggestions. For example, developers can enable intelligent code analysis and semantic parsing to provide more contextually relevant suggestions based on the semantics of the code being written. This advanced analysis allows code completion and suggestion tools to understand the meaning and intent behind the code, leading to more accurate and helpful recommendations.

Furthermore, code completion and suggestion tools can integrate with external libraries, frameworks, and APIs to provide even more comprehensive assistance to developers. For example, by analyzing project dependencies and imports, code completion tools can suggest relevant methods and classes from external libraries and frameworks, enabling developers to leverage third-party code seamlessly. Additionally, code completion tools can integrate with documentation sources and online resources to provide inline documentation and examples for suggested code snippets, further enhancing developers' understanding and productivity.

Deploying code completion and suggestion features typically involves configuring the code editor or IDE to enable these features and adjust their behavior and preferences as needed. For example, developers can customize the code completion triggers, suggestion thresholds, and filtering options to tailor the experience to their specific needs and coding style. Additionally, developers can install and configure plugins or extensions for their code editor to enhance its code completion and suggestion capabilities further.

As developers continue to use code completion and suggestion features in their coding sessions, they will become more familiar with their capabilities and learn to leverage them more effectively. By embracing these intelligent assistance tools, developers can streamline their development workflows, write better code more efficiently, and focus on solving higher-level problems and challenges. Ultimately, code completion and suggestions are indispensable tools for modern developers, empowering them to achieve greater productivity, code quality, and creativity in their software development endeavors.

Language support and integration are critical aspects of modern software development tools and platforms, enabling developers to work seamlessly across different programming languages and ecosystems. In today's diverse and rapidly evolving software landscape, developers often need to write code in multiple languages and frameworks to build robust and scalable applications. As such, having comprehensive language support and seamless integration capabilities is essential for ensuring productivity, efficiency, and compatibility across the entire development lifecycle.

One of the key considerations for developers when choosing a development tool or platform is its support for the programming languages and frameworks they use. Whether it's Java, Python, JavaScript, C++, or Ruby, developers rely on their preferred languages to express their ideas and implement their solutions effectively. Therefore, having robust language support in development tools and platforms is crucial for enabling developers to work comfortably and efficiently in their chosen languages. This includes features such as syntax highlighting, code completion, debugging support, and integration with language-specific tools and frameworks.

Deploying language support and integration often involves configuring the development environment to recognize and handle the syntax and semantics of different programming languages. For example, in a code editor like Visual Studio Code, developers can install language-specific extensions or plugins to enable syntax highlighting and code completion for different languages. Additionally, developers can configure the editor to use language servers or language-specific tools for features such as code navigation, refactoring, and documentation lookup. By customizing the development environment to support their preferred languages, developers can optimize their workflow and productivity.

Moreover, modern development platforms and frameworks often provide built-in support for multiple programming languages, enabling developers to build applications using a polyglot approach. For example, platforms like Node.js and .NET Core support multiple languages such as JavaScript, TypeScript, C#, and F#, allowing developers to choose the language that best suits their needs and preferences. This flexibility in language support enables developers to leverage their existing skills and expertise across different projects and domains, without being limited to a single language or ecosystem.

In addition to supporting individual programming languages, development tools and platforms also need to provide seamless integration with external libraries, frameworks, and APIs. For example, developers often rely on third-party libraries and frameworks to accelerate development, enhance functionality, and solve common problems. Therefore, having built-in support for package management, dependency resolution, and integration with package repositories such as npm, PyPI, and Maven is essential for enabling developers to leverage external code effectively.

Furthermore, integration with version control systems such as Git is crucial for enabling collaborative development workflows and ensuring code consistency and reliability. By integrating with Git repositories, development tools and platforms enable developers to perform version control operations such as committing changes, branching, merging, and resolving conflicts directly from the development environment. This tight integration streamlines the development process and facilitates seamless collaboration among team members, regardless of their location or time zone.

Deploying integration with version control systems often involves configuring the development environment to connect to the desired Git repository and authenticate with the appropriate credentials. For example, in a command-line interface (CLI) tool like Git, developers can use commands such as git clone, git pull, and git push to clone a repository, fetch the latest changes, and push local changes to the remote repository, respectively. Additionally, developers can configure Git to use authentication mechanisms such as SSH keys or personal access tokens to secure their interactions with remote repositories.

Another aspect of language support and integration is providing tools and services for continuous integration and continuous deployment (CI/CD). CI/CD pipelines enable developers to automate the process of building, testing, and deploying their applications, ensuring that code changes are integrated and delivered to production quickly and reliably. Development platforms often provide built-in support for popular CI/CD tools such as Jenkins, Travis CI, and GitHub Actions, allowing developers to configure and manage their CI/CD pipelines directly from the platform.

In summary, language support and integration are essential components of modern software development tools and platforms, enabling developers to work effectively across different programming languages and ecosystems. By providing comprehensive language support, seamless integration with external libraries and frameworks, and tools for version control, CI/CD, and collaboration, development platforms empower developers to build high-quality, scalable, and maintainable applications. As the software landscape continues to evolve, developers can expect to see further advancements in language support and integration, enabling them to stay productive and innovative in their software development endeavors.

Chapter 5: Basic Coding Tasks with Copilot

Generating code snippets with Copilot represents a significant advancement in the field of AI-assisted programming, offering developers a powerful tool for accelerating their coding workflows and enhancing productivity. GitHub Copilot, powered by OpenAI's GPT-3 model, leverages machine learning algorithms to analyze code contexts and generate contextually relevant code snippets in real-time. This innovative approach to code generation enables developers to automate repetitive coding tasks, explore new programming paradigms, and discover alternative solutions to complex problems.

Deploying Copilot for code snippet generation involves integrating the Copilot extension into a supported code editor, such as Visual Studio Code. Once installed, developers can activate Copilot within their coding environment and start leveraging its code generation capabilities. For example, when faced with a coding task or problem, developers can simply describe the desired functionality or behavior in plain language, and Copilot will generate code snippets based on the provided description. This intuitive interface allows developers to express their ideas and intentions naturally, without the need to write explicit code.

Furthermore, Copilot's code generation capabilities extend beyond simple code completion to include complex programming tasks and challenges. For instance, developers can use Copilot to generate entire functions, classes, or modules based on high-level specifications or requirements. By providing Copilot with input prompts or examples, developers can guide the code generation process and influence the quality and relevance of the generated code snippets. This collaborative approach to code generation empowers developers to work more efficiently and effectively, leveraging Copilot's AI-driven capabilities to augment their coding skills and expertise.

In addition to generating code snippets from scratch, Copilot can also assist developers with code refactoring and optimization tasks. For example, developers can use Copilot to identify redundant or inefficient code patterns and suggest alternative implementations or optimizations. By analyzing the code context and identifying opportunities for improvement, Copilot helps developers write cleaner, more maintainable code and adhere to coding standards and best practices.

Moreover, Copilot's code generation capabilities are not limited to a specific programming language or domain. Whether it's web development, machine learning, mobile app development, or system programming, Copilot can generate code snippets across a wide range of programming languages and frameworks. From JavaScript and Python to Java and C++, Copilot supports a diverse set of languages and ecosystems, enabling developers to leverage its code generation capabilities in virtually any development environment.

Deploying Copilot for code snippet generation is a seamless process that integrates into the developer's existing workflow. Once activated within the code editor, Copilot analyzes the code context and provides intelligent code suggestions and completions in real-time. Developers can interact with Copilot by accepting its suggestions, modifying the generated code as needed, and incorporating it into their projects. By seamlessly integrating Copilot into their coding environment, developers can leverage its AI-driven capabilities to accelerate their development workflows and write better code more efficiently.

Furthermore, Copilot's code generation capabilities are continuously improving and evolving over time. GitHub and OpenAI are actively collaborating to enhance Copilot's AI models and algorithms, enabling it to generate more accurate, relevant, and contextually appropriate code snippets. As Copilot learns from developers' interactions and feedback, it becomes more proficient at understanding code contexts, identifying patterns, and generating high-quality code snippets. This iterative improvement process ensures that Copilot remains a valuable and indispensable tool for developers, empowering them to tackle increasingly complex coding tasks with confidence.

In summary, generating code snippets with Copilot represents a groundbreaking advancement in AI-assisted programming, offering developers a powerful tool for accelerating their coding workflows and enhancing productivity. By leveraging machine learning algorithms to analyze code contexts and generate contextually relevant code snippets in real-time, Copilot enables developers to automate repetitive coding tasks, explore new programming paradigms, and discover alternative solutions to complex problems. As Copilot continues to evolve and improve, it will undoubtedly play an increasingly integral role in shaping the future of software development.

Solving simple programming challenges is an essential skill for developers at all levels, from beginners to seasoned professionals. These challenges, often presented as coding puzzles or exercises, help developers hone their problem-solving abilities, strengthen their understanding of programming concepts, and improve their coding proficiency. Whether it's finding the sum of an array, reversing a string, or implementing a basic sorting algorithm, simple programming challenges provide valuable opportunities for developers to practice their coding skills and gain confidence in tackling more complex problems.

To begin solving simple programming challenges, developers typically need access to a code editor or integrated development environment (IDE) where they can write and execute code. Popular code editors such as Visual Studio Code, Sublime Text, and Atom offer built-in support for various programming languages and provide features such as syntax highlighting, code completion, and debugging tools that facilitate the coding process. Once the code editor is set up, developers can create a new file or project to start working on the programming challenge.

In addition to a code editor, developers may also use online coding platforms or challenge websites that offer a curated selection of programming puzzles and exercises. These platforms provide a convenient way for developers to practice their coding skills, compete with others, and track their progress over time. Examples of popular coding platforms include LeetCode, HackerRank, and CodeSignal, which offer a wide range of programming challenges across different difficulty levels and domains.

When faced with a programming challenge, developers typically follow a systematic approach to devise a solution. This approach often involves breaking down the problem into smaller, more manageable subproblems, identifying relevant algorithms and data structures, and implementing the solution iteratively. For example, when tasked with finding the sum of an array, developers may start by initializing a variable to store the sum and then iterate through the array, adding each element to the sum. By breaking down the problem into smaller steps and tackling each step systematically, developers can develop a clear plan of action and implement an effective solution.

Moreover, developers often leverage existing algorithms and programming patterns to solve programming challenges more efficiently. For example, common algorithms such as binary search, merge sort, and dynamic programming are frequently used to solve a variety of programming problems across different domains. By understanding these algorithms and their underlying principles, developers can apply them creatively to solve new challenges and optimize their code for performance and scalability.

Deploying solutions to programming challenges typically involves writing code in the chosen programming language and testing it against a set of sample inputs or test cases. In a code editor or IDE, developers can write the code for their solution, incorporating any necessary algorithms, data structures, or helper functions. Once the code is written, developers can run it locally on their machine to verify that it produces the expected output for the given inputs. For example, in a command-line interface (CLI), developers can use commands such as gcc, javac, or python to compile or interpret their code and execute it with specific input parameters.

Additionally, developers may use version control systems such as Git to track changes to their code and collaborate with others on solving programming challenges. By using Git, developers can create a new branch for each programming challenge, commit their code changes incrementally, and push their branch to a remote repository for review and feedback. This collaborative workflow enables developers to work together efficiently and share insights and ideas for solving programming challenges effectively.

Furthermore, developers often seek out resources and communities for support and guidance when solving programming challenges. Online forums, discussion groups, and social media platforms provide valuable opportunities for developers to share their experiences, ask questions, and learn from others. By participating in these communities, developers can gain valuable insights into different approaches and techniques for solving programming challenges, expand their knowledge and skills, and connect with like-minded individuals who share their passion for coding.

In summary, solving simple programming challenges is a fundamental skill for developers that helps them improve their problem-solving abilities, strengthen their coding proficiency, and gain confidence in tackling more complex problems. By following a systematic approach, leveraging existing algorithms and programming patterns, and collaborating with others, developers can effectively solve programming challenges and continue to grow and evolve as programmers. Whether it's through practice on coding platforms, participation in online communities, or self-directed learning, developers can sharpen their skills and become more adept at solving programming challenges of all kinds.

Chapter 6: Navigating Copilot Suggestions

Understanding and evaluating Copilot suggestions is essential for developers looking to leverage this AI-powered tool effectively in their coding workflows. GitHub Copilot, powered by OpenAI's GPT-3 model, analyzes code contexts and generates contextually relevant suggestions to assist developers in their coding tasks. These suggestions can range from simple code completions to more complex code snippets, refactorings, and even entire functions or classes. However, to make the most of Copilot's capabilities, developers need to understand how to interpret and evaluate its suggestions accurately.

When evaluating Copilot suggestions, developers should consider several factors to determine their relevance, correctness, and suitability for the given context. One of the first considerations is the clarity and comprehensibility of the suggestion. Developers should ensure that the suggested code is easy to understand and aligns with the intended functionality and logic of the code being written. This involves checking for proper variable naming, logical structure, and adherence to coding conventions and best practices.

Additionally, developers should evaluate the accuracy and correctness of Copilot suggestions by reviewing the generated code for potential errors or inconsistencies. While Copilot strives to provide accurate and relevant suggestions based on the input context, it is not infallible, and there may be instances where the suggested code contains bugs or unintended behavior. Therefore, developers should carefully review and test Copilot suggestions to ensure their correctness before incorporating them into their projects.

To deploy Copilot suggestions in a coding environment, developers can interact with Copilot directly within their code editor or IDE. Once Copilot is activated, developers can start typing code as they normally would, and Copilot will provide suggestions in real-time based on the code context. Developers can then accept Copilot suggestions by selecting them from the suggestion list or pressing the corresponding keyboard shortcut provided by the editor.

Moreover, developers should evaluate the efficiency and effectiveness of Copilot suggestions in terms of their impact on code quality and development productivity. Copilot suggestions should not only help developers write code faster but also improve the overall quality and maintainability of the codebase. Developers should assess whether the suggested code adheres to coding standards, minimizes code duplication, and follows established design principles and patterns.

Furthermore, developers should consider the scalability and extensibility of Copilot suggestions in the context of their projects and development workflows. While Copilot can generate code snippets and solutions for a wide range of programming tasks and challenges, developers should evaluate whether the suggested code integrates seamlessly with existing codebases, libraries, and frameworks. Additionally, developers should assess whether the suggested code is easily adaptable and extensible to accommodate future changes and requirements.

Another important aspect to consider when evaluating Copilot suggestions is their potential impact on code security and reliability. Developers should be cautious when incorporating third-party code generated by Copilot into their projects, especially when dealing with sensitive or critical systems. While Copilot strives to generate secure and reliable code, developers should perform thorough code reviews, security audits, and testing to ensure that the suggested code meets the required standards for security and reliability.

Additionally, developers should be mindful of potential legal and ethical considerations when using Copilot suggestions in their projects. Copilot generates code based on a vast corpus of code from publicly available sources, which may include copyrighted or proprietary code. Therefore, developers should ensure that they have the necessary rights and permissions to use the suggested code in their projects and comply with applicable licensing agreements and intellectual property laws.

In summary, understanding and evaluating Copilot suggestions is essential for developers to leverage this AI-powered tool effectively in their coding workflows. By considering factors such as clarity, accuracy, efficiency, scalability, security, and legal considerations, developers can make informed decisions about incorporating Copilot suggestions into their projects. With careful evaluation and testing, developers can harness the power of Copilot to write better code more efficiently and advance their software development endeavors.

Refining suggestions for specific tasks is a crucial aspect of utilizing AI-powered tools like GitHub Copilot effectively in software development. While Copilot's suggestions are generally accurate and helpful, refining them for specific tasks allows developers to tailor the suggestions to their unique requirements, improve code quality, and ensure alignment with project objectives. Whether it's customizing code snippets for a particular programming language, optimizing performance for a specific platform, or adhering to coding standards and best practices, refining Copilot suggestions enables developers to achieve better results and enhance their coding productivity.

When refining suggestions for specific tasks, developers should start by clearly defining the requirements and constraints of the task at hand. This involves understanding the desired functionality, performance goals, and compatibility requirements of the code being developed. By establishing clear objectives and criteria for success, developers can guide Copilot's suggestions more effectively and ensure that the generated code meets the project's needs.

To refine Copilot suggestions for specific tasks, developers can leverage various techniques and strategies depending on the nature of the task and the desired outcome. One approach is to provide additional context or constraints to Copilot by incorporating comments or annotations directly into the code. For example, developers can add comments to indicate specific requirements or preferences for the generated code, such as performance optimizations, error handling strategies, or compatibility considerations.

Additionally, developers can refine Copilot suggestions by adjusting the input context or query used to generate the suggestions. By providing more detailed or specific input to Copilot, developers can guide the code generation process and influence the quality and relevance of the suggestions. For example, developers can modify the prompt or query given to Copilot to include additional keywords, examples, or constraints related to the task, thereby directing Copilot's attention to the relevant aspects of the code.

Furthermore, developers can refine Copilot suggestions by iteratively testing and validating the generated code against a set of sample inputs or test cases. This iterative feedback loop allows developers to identify and address potential issues or shortcomings in the suggested code, such as edge cases, performance bottlenecks, or compatibility issues. By continuously refining and testing Copilot suggestions, developers can iteratively improve the quality and reliability of the generated code and ensure that it meets the project's requirements.

Deploying refined Copilot suggestions often involves integrating the generated code into the existing codebase and adapting it to fit the project's architecture and coding conventions. For example, developers may need to refactor or modify the generated code to align with established design patterns, naming conventions, and coding standards used in the project. Additionally, developers may need to test and debug the refined code to ensure that it behaves as expected and integrates smoothly with other components of the system.

Moreover, developers can refine Copilot suggestions by incorporating feedback and insights from code reviews, peer collaboration, and domain experts. By soliciting input from team members and stakeholders, developers can gain valuable perspectives and identify opportunities for improvement in the generated code. This collaborative approach to refining Copilot suggestions fosters a culture of continuous learning and improvement within the development team and ensures that the generated code meets the highest standards of quality and reliability.

Another technique for refining Copilot suggestions is to customize the code generation settings and preferences within the code editor or IDE. For example, developers can adjust the code completion triggers, suggestion thresholds, and filtering options to fine-tune Copilot's behavior and improve the relevance and accuracy of the suggestions. Additionally, developers can configure Copilot to use specific coding styles, libraries, or frameworks preferred by the project or organization, ensuring consistency and coherence across the codebase.

Furthermore, developers can refine Copilot suggestions by leveraging advanced programming techniques and patterns to optimize the generated code for performance, scalability, and maintainability. For example, developers can apply algorithms and data structures to improve the efficiency of the generated code, refactor code to reduce complexity and increase readability, and apply design patterns to promote code reuse and modularity. By applying these advanced techniques, developers can enhance the quality and robustness of the generated code and ensure that it meets the project's requirements and objectives.

In summary, refining suggestions for specific tasks is a critical aspect of leveraging GitHub Copilot effectively in software development. By clearly defining task requirements, providing additional context or constraints, iteratively testing and validating suggestions, integrating feedback from stakeholders, customizing code generation settings, and applying advanced programming techniques, developers can refine Copilot suggestions to meet the unique needs of their projects. With careful refinement and testing, developers can harness the power of Copilot to write better code more efficiently and advance their software development endeavors.

Chapter 7: Customizing Copilot for Your Workflow

Personalizing Copilot settings is essential for developers to tailor the AI-powered tool to their individual preferences, coding style, and project requirements. GitHub Copilot offers various customization options and settings that allow developers to adjust its behavior, suggestions, and interactions within their coding environment. By personalizing Copilot settings, developers can optimize their coding experience, improve productivity, and ensure that Copilot aligns with their specific needs and workflows.

To personalize Copilot settings, developers can start by accessing the settings menu within their code editor or IDE. In Visual Studio Code, for example, developers can navigate to File > Preferences > Settings and search for "Copilot" to find the relevant settings options. Once in the Copilot settings menu, developers can explore the available customization options and adjust them according to their preferences.

One of the key settings that developers can personalize is the code completion trigger for Copilot suggestions. By default, Copilot provides suggestions automatically as developers type code in their editor. However, developers can choose to change the trigger behavior to require a specific key combination, such as pressing the Tab key or a custom keyboard shortcut, to invoke Copilot suggestions. This allows developers to control when and how Copilot suggestions appear, reducing distractions and ensuring a more focused coding experience.

Additionally, developers can personalize Copilot settings related to the types of suggestions and completions that Copilot provides. For example, developers can enable or disable specific programming languages or frameworks for which Copilot generates suggestions. This allows developers to tailor Copilot's suggestions to the languages and technologies they use most frequently and filter out irrelevant suggestions for languages they do not use.

Moreover, developers can personalize Copilot settings to adjust the frequency and aggressiveness of suggestions based on their coding preferences. For example, developers can adjust the suggestion threshold to control how often Copilot provides suggestions, ranging from conservative to aggressive. By fine-tuning this setting, developers can strike a balance between receiving helpful suggestions and avoiding unnecessary distractions during coding sessions.

Furthermore, developers can personalize Copilot settings to customize the appearance and behavior of Copilot suggestions within their code editor or IDE. For example, developers can adjust the font size, color scheme, and display mode for Copilot suggestions to make them more visually distinct and easier to identify. Additionally, developers can customize the behavior of Copilot suggestions, such as enabling or disabling automatic insertion of suggestions and adjusting the formatting options for inserted code snippets.

Deploying personalized Copilot settings involves configuring the desired options within the code editor or IDE and saving the changes to apply them to future coding sessions. Once the settings are configured to their liking, developers can start using Copilot with their personalized preferences and enjoy a more tailored and efficient coding experience. By regularly reviewing and adjusting Copilot settings based on their evolving needs and preferences, developers can optimize their use of the tool and maximize its effectiveness in their coding workflows.

Another aspect of personalizing Copilot settings is configuring the privacy and data usage preferences for the tool. Copilot relies on machine learning algorithms and models trained on vast amounts of code data to generate suggestions. While Copilot strives to protect user privacy and confidentiality, developers may have specific preferences or concerns regarding data usage and privacy. Therefore, developers can personalize Copilot settings to adjust data sharing and telemetry options, such as opting in or out of sharing usage data with GitHub for research and improvement purposes.

Furthermore, developers can personalize Copilot settings to incorporate their coding style and preferences into the suggestions generated by the tool. For example, developers can specify preferred coding conventions, naming conventions, and formatting preferences to ensure that Copilot suggestions align with their coding standards and practices. By customizing these settings, developers can ensure consistency and coherence in the code generated by Copilot and seamlessly integrate it into their projects.

Additionally, developers can personalize Copilot settings to incorporate domain-specific knowledge and vocabulary into the suggestions provided by the tool. For example, developers working in specialized domains such as finance, healthcare, or gaming may have specific terminology, APIs, and design patterns unique to their field. By customizing Copilot settings to include domain-specific terms and concepts, developers can enhance the relevance and accuracy of the suggestions generated by the tool and streamline their coding process.

In summary, personalizing Copilot settings is essential for developers to optimize their use of the AI-powered tool and tailor it to their individual preferences and requirements. By adjusting settings related to code completion triggers, suggestion types, suggestion frequency, appearance, behavior, privacy preferences, coding style, and domain-specific knowledge, developers can create a personalized coding experience that enhances productivity and efficiency. With personalized Copilot settings, developers can harness the power of AI to write better code more efficiently and advance their software development endeavors.

Creating custom code templates and shortcuts is a valuable practice for developers seeking to streamline their coding workflows, improve productivity, and maintain consistency in their codebases. Code templates, also known as snippets or boilerplate code, are pre-defined chunks of code that can be easily inserted into a code editor or IDE to automate repetitive coding tasks and provide scaffolding for common programming patterns. Shortcuts, on the other hand, are keyboard commands or sequences that trigger specific actions or commands within the coding environment, such as inserting code snippets, executing commands, or navigating code files. By creating custom code templates and shortcuts tailored to their specific needs and preferences, developers can speed up their coding process, reduce manual effort, and focus more on solving complex problems and implementing innovative solutions.

To create custom code templates and shortcuts, developers can leverage the built-in features and extensibility mechanisms provided by their code editor or IDE. For example, in Visual Studio Code, developers can create custom snippets using the built-in snippet functionality or by installing extensions such as "Snippet Generator" or "Custom Snippets." Similarly, in Sublime Text, developers can define custom snippets using the built-in snippet syntax or by creating snippet files in the appropriate directory.

One approach to creating custom code templates is to identify recurring patterns or code structures in your projects and extract them into reusable snippets. For example, if you frequently write code to define classes or functions with specific boilerplate code, you can create a custom snippet that inserts the necessary code with placeholders for variable names or parameters. This allows you to quickly generate common code structures without having to type them out manually each time.

Moreover, developers can create custom code templates for specific programming languages, frameworks, or libraries to streamline development in those contexts. For example, if you frequently work with React.js, you can create custom snippets for common React components or lifecycle methods to accelerate development. Similarly, if you're working on a project that uses a specific coding style or design pattern, you can create custom snippets that adhere to those conventions and ensure consistency across your codebase.

Deploying custom code templates involves configuring the code editor or IDE to recognize and use the custom snippets in your projects. In Visual Studio Code, for example, you can create a new snippet file or modify an existing one to define your custom snippets. Once the snippets are defined, you can save the file and specify the scope or language for which the snippets should be available. The code editor will then automatically recognize the custom snippets and make them available for insertion using the specified trigger keyword or shortcut.

In addition to creating custom code templates, developers can also create custom shortcuts or keybindings to streamline common tasks and actions within the coding environment. For example, you can define keyboard shortcuts to insert specific code snippets, execute frequently used commands, or navigate code files more efficiently. By assigning intuitive and memorable shortcuts to these actions, you can save time and reduce cognitive load when working on complex coding tasks.

One common technique for creating custom shortcuts is to use the built-in keybinding customization features provided by your code editor or IDE. For example, in Visual Studio Code, you can open the Keyboard Shortcuts settings and define new keybindings for various commands and actions. You can specify the key combination, command name, and context in which the shortcut should be active, such as the editor, terminal, or debugging session. Once the custom shortcuts are defined, you can start using them immediately to streamline your coding workflow.

Furthermore, developers can create custom shortcuts for specific plugins or extensions installed in their code editor or IDE. Many plugins and extensions provide customizable keybindings that allow you to define shortcuts for their features and functionalities. For example, if you're using a Git integration plugin, you can create custom shortcuts for common Git commands such as committing changes, pushing to a remote repository, or switching branches. By assigning shortcuts to these actions, you can perform them quickly and efficiently without leaving your coding environment.

Another approach to creating custom shortcuts is to use external tools or scripts to automate repetitive tasks or workflows. For example, you can create shell scripts or batch files that execute a series of commands or tasks, such as building a project, running tests, or deploying code to a server. You can then create custom shortcuts or aliases in your terminal shell to invoke these scripts with a single command. This allows you to automate complex tasks and workflows and execute them with minimal effort from the command line.

In summary, creating custom code templates and shortcuts is a powerful technique for streamlining coding workflows, improving productivity, and maintaining consistency in codebases. By identifying recurring patterns and tasks in your projects and creating custom snippets and shortcuts to automate them, you can save time, reduce manual effort, and focus more on solving complex problems and implementing innovative solutions. Whether you're creating custom snippets for common code structures or defining shortcuts for frequently used commands and actions, customizing your coding environment to fit your needs and preferences can significantly enhance your coding experience and efficiency.

Chapter 8: Collaborating with GitHub Copilot

Pair programming with Copilot is an innovative approach that combines the collaborative benefits of pair programming with the AI-powered assistance of GitHub Copilot. Pair programming, a practice where two developers work together at a single workstation, has long been recognized for its ability to improve code quality, enhance problem-solving skills, and foster knowledge sharing and collaboration within development teams. GitHub Copilot, on the other hand, leverages advanced machine learning models to provide intelligent code suggestions and assistance based on the context of the code being written. By combining the strengths of pair programming with the capabilities of Copilot, developers can collaborate more effectively, leverage the collective expertise of both human and AI partners, and accelerate the software development process.

To engage in pair programming with Copilot, developers typically work in pairs using a shared code editor or IDE that supports real-time collaboration. Tools such as Visual Studio Code's Live Share extension or Google's Cloud-based Collaborative Development Environment (CDE) provide features for collaborative editing, code sharing, and real-time communication, enabling developers to work together seamlessly regardless of their physical location. Once the collaborative environment is set up, developers can invite their pair to join the coding session and start working together on a shared codebase.

During a pair programming session with Copilot, developers take turns writing code and reviewing Copilot suggestions to assist them in their coding tasks. The developer who is not actively typing, known as the navigator, observes the code being written and provides feedback, suggestions, and guidance to the driver, who is responsible for writing the code. As the driver writes code, Copilot analyzes the code context and generates relevant suggestions, such as code completions, refactorings, or entire code snippets, to assist the driver in their coding tasks.

One of the key benefits of pair programming with Copilot is the ability to leverage the collective expertise of both human and AI partners to solve coding challenges more effectively. While Copilot can provide intelligent suggestions and assistance based on its vast knowledge of programming patterns and best practices, human developers bring domain expertise, creativity, and problem-solving skills to the table. By working together, developers can complement each other's strengths and weaknesses, validate Copilot suggestions, and ensure that the generated code meets the project's requirements and objectives.

Moreover, pair programming with Copilot facilitates knowledge sharing and skill development within development teams. As developers collaborate on coding tasks and review Copilot suggestions together, they have opportunities to learn from each other, share insights and best practices, and improve their coding proficiency. Junior developers can benefit from the guidance and mentorship of more experienced developers, while senior developers can gain new perspectives and insights from junior developers, creating a culture of continuous learning and growth within the team.

Deploying pair programming with Copilot involves setting up the collaborative coding environment, inviting your pair to join the session, and establishing effective communication and collaboration practices. Once the pair programming session is underway, developers can leverage Copilot suggestions to streamline coding tasks, accelerate development, and improve code quality. By actively engaging in code review and discussion, developers can ensure that the generated code meets the project's requirements, adheres to coding standards, and aligns with the overall design and architecture of the codebase.

Furthermore, pair programming with Copilot promotes teamwork, collaboration, and accountability within development teams. By working together on coding tasks and sharing responsibility for writing and reviewing code, developers build trust, camaraderie, and mutual respect within the team. Pair programming fosters a sense of collective ownership of the codebase and encourages developers to take pride in their work, leading to higher levels of engagement, motivation, and job satisfaction.

Another benefit of pair programming with Copilot is its potential to improve code quality and maintainability. By leveraging Copilot's intelligent suggestions and incorporating feedback from pair programming partners, developers can write cleaner, more readable, and more maintainable code. Pair programming encourages developers to adhere to coding standards, follow established design patterns, and refactor code as needed to improve its structure, clarity, and extensibility. As a result, the codebase becomes more robust, resilient, and easier to maintain over time.

Moreover, pair programming with Copilot enhances problem-solving skills and creativity among developers. By collaboratively tackling coding challenges and brainstorming solutions together, developers can explore different approaches, experiment with new ideas, and push the boundaries of what is possible. Pair programming encourages developers to think critically, communicate effectively, and iterate on solutions until they find the most optimal and elegant solution to the problem at hand.

In summary, pair programming with Copilot is a powerful technique for enhancing collaboration, accelerating development, and improving code quality within development teams. By combining the strengths of pair programming with the intelligent assistance of Copilot, developers can leverage the collective expertise of both human and AI partners to solve coding challenges more effectively, foster knowledge sharing and skill development, and create a culture of teamwork, innovation, and excellence within the team. With its ability to promote collaboration, improve code quality, and enhance problem-solving skills, pair programming with Copilot is poised to revolutionize the way developers work together and build software in the modern era.

Integrating Copilot into team workflows is a strategic endeavor that requires careful planning, collaboration, and adaptation to ensure smooth adoption and maximize the benefits of the AI-powered tool within the development process. GitHub Copilot, with its ability to provide intelligent code suggestions and assistance based on the context of the code being written, has the potential to streamline development, improve code quality, and enhance collaboration within development teams. However, successful integration of Copilot into team workflows requires consideration of various factors, including team dynamics, project requirements, coding standards, and communication practices, to ensure that the tool complements existing processes and facilitates productive collaboration among team members.

To integrate Copilot into team workflows, teams should first assess their current development processes, tools, and practices to identify areas where Copilot can add value and improve efficiency. This involves evaluating the team's coding workflows, communication channels, version control practices, and collaboration tools to understand how Copilot can fit into the existing ecosystem and support team objectives. Teams should also consider the skill levels and familiarity of team members with Copilot and provide training and resources as needed to ensure that everyone can effectively leverage the tool in their work.

Once the team has assessed its needs and identified opportunities for integrating Copilot into its workflows, the next step is to establish guidelines, best practices, and standards for using the tool effectively. This includes defining roles and responsibilities within the team, establishing coding conventions and standards, and outlining communication protocols for collaborating with Copilot. Teams should also establish mechanisms for monitoring and evaluating the impact of Copilot on development processes and code quality and iterate on their workflows based on feedback and lessons learned.

Deploying Copilot within team workflows involves configuring the tool to align with team preferences, integrating it with existing development tools and processes, and ensuring that team members have access to the necessary resources and support to use the tool effectively. This may include installing Copilot extensions or plugins for code editors or IDEs, configuring settings and preferences to match team coding standards, and integrating Copilot with version control systems such as Git for seamless collaboration and code review.

One approach to integrating Copilot into team workflows is to incorporate it into the code review process as part of the peer review workflow. During code reviews, team members can leverage Copilot suggestions to provide feedback, suggest improvements, and identify potential issues in the code being reviewed. By leveraging Copilot's intelligent assistance, teams can expedite the code review process, improve code quality, and facilitate knowledge sharing and collaboration among team members.

Moreover, teams can integrate Copilot into their coding workflows by incorporating it into pair programming sessions, hackathons, or collaborative coding sessions. Pair programming with Copilot enables developers to work together in real-time, leverage Copilot suggestions to streamline coding tasks, and share knowledge and expertise to solve coding challenges more effectively. Similarly, hackathons or collaborative coding sessions provide opportunities for team members to experiment with Copilot, explore new ideas, and prototype solutions collaboratively.

In addition to integrating Copilot into coding workflows, teams can leverage Copilot's capabilities to automate repetitive coding tasks, accelerate development, and improve productivity. By creating custom code templates, snippets, or shortcuts using Copilot, teams can standardize coding patterns, reduce manual effort, and ensure consistency across codebases. Teams can also leverage Copilot to generate documentation, unit tests, or other auxiliary artifacts to complement their development efforts and improve code maintainability and reliability.

Furthermore, integrating Copilot into team workflows can enhance communication and collaboration among team members by providing a shared context and reference point for discussing code and sharing insights and ideas. By incorporating Copilot suggestions into code reviews, discussions, and brainstorming sessions, teams can foster a culture of collaboration, innovation, and continuous improvement within the team. Teams can also use Copilot to document coding decisions, capture knowledge, and share best practices to facilitate onboarding of new team members and promote knowledge sharing and transfer within the team.

In summary, integrating Copilot into team workflows is a strategic initiative that requires careful planning, collaboration, and adaptation to ensure successful adoption and maximize the benefits of the AI-powered tool within the development process. By assessing team needs, establishing guidelines and best practices, deploying Copilot effectively, and leveraging its capabilities to streamline development, improve code quality, and enhance collaboration, teams can harness the full potential of Copilot to accelerate their software development efforts and achieve their objectives. With its ability to facilitate communication, collaboration, and innovation, Copilot has the potential to transform the way teams work together and build software in the modern era.

Chapter 9: Best Practices for Using Copilot Effectively

Maximizing efficiency with Copilot is a crucial goal for developers aiming to optimize their coding workflows, improve productivity, and deliver high-quality software solutions efficiently. GitHub Copilot, powered by advanced machine learning algorithms, offers intelligent code suggestions and assistance based on the context of the code being written, enabling developers to streamline coding tasks, reduce manual effort, and accelerate development cycles. By leveraging Copilot effectively, developers can unlock new levels of efficiency, creativity, and innovation in their software development endeavors.

To maximize efficiency with Copilot, developers must first familiarize themselves with the capabilities and features of the tool and learn how to leverage its intelligent assistance to streamline their coding workflows. This involves exploring Copilot's code suggestion capabilities, understanding how it analyzes code context to provide relevant suggestions, and learning how to interact with Copilot effectively within their code editor or IDE. By mastering Copilot's features and functionalities, developers can harness its full potential to optimize their coding process and maximize efficiency.

Deploying Copilot in the development workflow involves integrating the tool into the code editor or IDE used by the development team and configuring its settings and preferences to align with team coding standards and preferences. In Visual Studio Code, for example, developers can install the Copilot extension from the Visual Studio Code marketplace and configure settings such as code completion triggers, suggestion behavior, and language support to enhance their coding experience. By customizing Copilot settings to suit their individual preferences and requirements, developers can ensure a seamless integration of the tool into their development workflow.

One strategy for maximizing efficiency with Copilot is to leverage its code suggestion capabilities to automate repetitive coding tasks and accelerate development. Copilot can generate intelligent code completions, refactorings, and code snippets based on the context of the code being written, enabling developers to write code more quickly and efficiently. By using Copilot to automate common coding patterns, developers can reduce manual effort, minimize errors, and focus their attention on solving more complex problems and implementing innovative solutions.

Moreover, developers can use Copilot to explore new coding techniques, experiment with different programming paradigms, and prototype solutions quickly and iteratively. Copilot's ability to generate intelligent code suggestions based on the context of the code being written allows developers to explore alternative approaches, refactor code easily, and test hypotheses in real-time. By leveraging Copilot's assistance to prototype and iterate on solutions rapidly, developers can accelerate the development cycle, iterate more quickly, and deliver high-quality software solutions faster.

Additionally, teams can maximize efficiency with Copilot by incorporating it into collaborative coding sessions, pair programming sessions, or hackathons. By working together in real-time and leveraging Copilot's intelligent assistance, developers can collaborate more effectively, share knowledge and expertise, and solve coding challenges more efficiently. Pair programming with Copilot enables developers to work together to write code, review suggestions, and provide feedback in real-time, leading to faster development cycles, improved code quality, and enhanced collaboration within the team.

Another strategy for maximizing efficiency with Copilot is to create custom code templates, snippets, or shortcuts using Copilot's capabilities. By defining reusable code patterns, boilerplate code, or common coding idioms as custom snippets or templates, developers can standardize coding practices, reduce duplication of effort, and ensure consistency across codebases. Moreover, by creating custom shortcuts or aliases for common Copilot commands or actions, developers can streamline their coding workflows, minimize manual effort, and improve productivity.

Furthermore, developers can maximize efficiency with Copilot by leveraging its capabilities to generate documentation, unit tests, or other auxiliary artifacts to complement their development efforts. Copilot can assist developers in writing documentation, generating test cases, or implementing error handling logic based on the context of the code being written, enabling developers to maintain code quality, reliability, and maintainability. By automating the generation of documentation and tests with Copilot, developers can reduce overhead, improve code coverage, and ensure that their software solutions are robust and reliable.

In summary, maximizing efficiency with Copilot requires developers to leverage its intelligent assistance, explore its capabilities, and integrate it effectively into their coding workflows. By deploying Copilot in the development workflow, automating repetitive coding tasks, exploring new coding techniques, collaborating effectively with team members, and creating custom code templates and shortcuts, developers can unlock new levels of efficiency, productivity, and innovation in their software development endeavors. With its ability to streamline coding tasks, accelerate development cycles, and improve code quality, Copilot has the potential to revolutionize the way developers work and deliver software solutions in the modern era.

Avoiding common pitfalls and misuse of tools is essential for developers seeking to maximize the benefits of GitHub Copilot while minimizing potential risks and challenges in their coding workflows. While Copilot offers valuable assistance in generating code suggestions and automating coding tasks, it is essential to understand its limitations, potential pitfalls, and best practices for effective and responsible use. By being mindful of common pitfalls and adopting best practices, developers can ensure that Copilot enhances their productivity, code quality, and collaboration without introducing unnecessary complexity or issues into their projects.

One common pitfall when using Copilot is over-reliance on its code suggestions without understanding the underlying principles or logic behind the generated code. While Copilot can provide intelligent suggestions based on the context of the code being written, blindly accepting its suggestions without critical evaluation can lead to code that is inefficient, insecure, or difficult to maintain. To avoid this pitfall, developers should take the time to review and understand Copilot suggestions, validate them against project requirements and coding standards, and modify them as needed to ensure that the generated code meets their specific needs.

Deploying Copilot effectively also requires careful consideration of licensing and copyright implications, especially when using Copilot to generate code for proprietary or commercial projects. While Copilot's code suggestions are based on a vast corpus of open-source code available on GitHub, developers should be mindful of licensing restrictions and ensure that the generated code complies with the licensing terms of the original code snippets. Additionally, developers should avoid using Copilot to generate code that infringes on third-party intellectual property rights or violates copyright laws to mitigate legal risks and potential liabilities.

Moreover, developers should be cautious when using Copilot to generate code for security-sensitive or mission-critical applications, as the tool may not always produce secure or reliable code by default. While

Copilot can assist in automating coding tasks and accelerating development, developers should exercise caution when using it to handle sensitive data, implement security-critical functionalities, or interact with external systems. To mitigate security risks, developers should review and validate Copilot suggestions carefully, conduct thorough testing and security analysis, and follow established best practices for secure coding and application security.

Another common pitfall when using Copilot is relying too heavily on its suggestions without actively engaging in problem-solving or critical thinking. While Copilot can provide valuable assistance in generating code snippets and automating coding tasks, developers should view it as a tool to augment their coding skills and expertise rather than a replacement for human intelligence. To avoid falling into this trap, developers should approach Copilot suggestions critically, evaluate them in the context of the problem being solved, and use them as a starting point for further exploration and refinement.

Furthermore, developers should be mindful of potential biases and limitations in Copilot's training data and machine learning models, which may affect the quality and relevance of its code suggestions. Like any AI-powered tool, Copilot's suggestions are based on patterns and examples present in its training data, which may reflect biases or limitations inherent in the data sources or algorithms used to train the models. To mitigate the risk of biased or irrelevant suggestions, developers should review and validate Copilot suggestions carefully, consider alternative approaches, and seek input from diverse perspectives when making coding decisions.

Additionally, developers should be aware of performance considerations when using Copilot in resource-constrained environments or on large codebases. While Copilot's code suggestions are generated quickly and efficiently, they may consume significant computational resources or introduce performance overhead when processing large code files or complex code patterns. To optimize performance, developers should monitor the resource usage of Copilot within their development environment, profile code execution to identify potential bottlenecks, and adopt strategies to mitigate performance issues as needed.

In summary, avoiding common pitfalls and misuse of GitHub Copilot requires developers to approach the tool with caution, critical thinking, and an understanding of its capabilities and limitations. By being mindful of licensing and copyright implications, exercising caution when handling security-sensitive code, engaging in problem-solving and critical thinking, being aware of potential biases and limitations, and considering performance considerations, developers can leverage Copilot effectively to enhance their productivity, code quality, and collaboration within development teams. With responsible use and careful consideration of best practices, Copilot can be a valuable asset in the developer's toolkit, enabling them to tackle coding challenges more efficiently and effectively in the modern era.

Chapter 10: Future Developments in AI-Assisted Programming

Advancements in AI and machine learning have revolutionized various aspects of programming, offering developers powerful tools and techniques to streamline their workflows, improve code quality, and accelerate development cycles. From intelligent code completion and suggestion systems to automated code generation and refactoring tools, AI and machine learning technologies are reshaping the way developers write, review, and maintain code in the modern era.

One significant advancement in AI and machine learning for programming is the development of intelligent code completion and suggestion systems, such as GitHub Copilot, TabNine, and Kite, which leverage advanced natural language processing (NLP) and deep learning techniques to provide context-aware code suggestions and assistance to developers as they write code. These systems analyze the code context, including variable names, function signatures, and code patterns, to generate relevant code completions, refactorings, or entire code snippets in real-time, enabling developers to write code more quickly and efficiently.

Deploying AI-powered code completion and suggestion systems typically involves integrating them into the developer's preferred code editor or integrated development environment (IDE) and configuring their settings and preferences to align with individual coding styles and preferences. In Visual Studio Code, for example, developers can install the Copilot or TabNine extensions from the Visual Studio Code marketplace and configure settings such as completion triggers, suggestion behavior, and language support to enhance their coding experience.

Another area of advancement in AI and machine learning for programming is automated code generation and refactoring, which involves using AI-powered tools to automatically generate code snippets, refactor existing code, or optimize code performance based on predefined rules or learned patterns. Tools like DeepCode and CodeGuru use machine learning models trained on vast repositories of code to identify code smells, performance bottlenecks, or security vulnerabilities and suggest automated refactorings or optimizations to improve code quality and maintainability.

Using automated code generation and refactoring tools typically involves integrating them into the developer's development workflow and leveraging their capabilities to identify potential issues or inefficiencies in the codebase and suggest automated solutions or optimizations. Developers can use CLI commands or APIs provided by these tools to analyze code repositories, detect code smells or vulnerabilities, and apply automated refactorings or optimizations to improve code quality and performance.

Furthermore, advancements in AI and machine learning have enabled the development of intelligent bug detection and code review systems, such as CodeQL and DeepCode, which use static analysis and pattern recognition techniques to identify bugs, security vulnerabilities, or code style violations in code repositories and provide actionable feedback to developers. These systems analyze code patterns, control flow, and data flow within the codebase to detect potential issues and suggest fixes or improvements to ensure code quality and reliability.

Using intelligent bug detection and code review systems typically involves integrating them into the developer's continuous integration and continuous deployment (CI/CD) pipeline and configuring them to automatically analyze code changes and provide feedback to developers as part of the code review process. Developers can use CLI commands or APIs provided by these systems to run static analysis on code repositories, detect potential issues or vulnerabilities, and incorporate feedback into their development workflow to ensure code quality and reliability.

Moreover, advancements in AI and machine learning have facilitated the development of intelligent testing and test generation tools, such as EvoSuite and Diffblue, which use evolutionary algorithms and symbolic execution techniques to automatically generate test cases, identify edge cases, or generate test assertions based on code coverage metrics or test specifications. These tools help developers automate the testing process, improve test coverage, and ensure code correctness and robustness.

Using intelligent testing and test generation tools typically involves integrating them into the developer's testing framework or CI/CD pipeline and leveraging their capabilities to automatically generate test cases or test assertions based on code changes or coverage metrics. Developers can use CLI commands or APIs provided by these tools to analyze code repositories, generate test cases, and execute tests as part of the automated testing process to ensure code correctness and robustness.

Furthermore, advancements in AI and machine learning have led to the development of intelligent code summarization and documentation generation tools, such as DeepTabNine and Co-Pilot, which use natural language processing and machine learning techniques to automatically generate code summaries, documentation, or comments based on code snippets or function signatures. These tools help developers streamline the documentation process, improve code readability, and facilitate knowledge sharing and collaboration within development teams.

Using intelligent code summarization and documentation generation tools typically involves integrating them into the developer's code editor or IDE and configuring their settings and preferences to align with individual coding styles and preferences. Developers can use CLI commands or APIs provided by these tools to generate code summaries, documentation, or comments for code snippets or functions and incorporate them into their codebase to improve code readability and maintainability.

In summary, advancements in AI and machine learning have transformed various aspects of programming, offering developers powerful tools and techniques to streamline their workflows, improve code quality, and accelerate development cycles. From intelligent code completion and suggestion systems to automated code generation and refactoring tools, AI and machine learning technologies are reshaping the way developers write, review, and maintain code in the modern era. By leveraging these advancements effectively, developers can enhance their productivity, code quality, and collaboration within development teams, driving innovation and success in software development projects.

Understanding the potential impacts and ethical considerations of emerging technologies, such as AI and machine learning, is crucial for developers, policymakers, and society as a whole as these technologies continue to evolve and become increasingly integrated into our daily lives. While AI and machine learning offer tremendous potential to transform industries, improve efficiency, and drive innovation, they also raise significant ethical concerns related to privacy, bias, transparency, accountability, and societal impact that must be addressed to ensure responsible and ethical use of these technologies.

One potential impact of AI and machine learning is their ability to automate repetitive tasks, optimize processes, and improve productivity across various industries and sectors. By leveraging AI-powered tools and techniques, developers can streamline their workflows, reduce manual effort, and accelerate development cycles, leading to increased efficiency, faster time-to-market, and improved competitiveness for organizations. For example, using automated code completion and suggestion systems like GitHub Copilot can help developers write code more quickly and efficiently, leading to higher productivity and better code quality.

Deploying AI and machine learning techniques typically involves integrating them into existing systems, applications, or workflows and configuring them to suit specific use cases or requirements. For example, developers can use CLI commands or APIs provided by AI-powered tools to analyze data, train machine learning models, or automate coding tasks as part of their development process. By integrating AI and machine learning into their workflows, developers can unlock new capabilities, improve efficiency, and drive innovation in their projects.

However, the widespread adoption of AI and machine learning also raises ethical concerns related to data privacy, security, and fairness that must be addressed to ensure responsible and ethical use of these technologies. For example, AI-powered systems may rely on large amounts of data to train machine learning models, raising concerns about data privacy, consent, and ownership. Developers must ensure that they have the necessary permissions and rights to use data for training purposes and comply with relevant data protection regulations to protect user privacy and confidentiality.

Moreover, AI and machine learning algorithms may inadvertently perpetuate biases present in training data or introduce new biases based on algorithmic decisions, leading to unfair or discriminatory outcomes. For example, AI-powered hiring tools may inadvertently discriminate against certain demographic groups based on biased training data or flawed algorithmic decisions. Developers must be mindful of biases in training data, algorithms, and decision-making processes and take steps to mitigate bias and ensure fairness and equity in AI-powered systems.

Addressing ethical considerations in AI and machine learning requires a multidisciplinary approach involving developers, ethicists, policymakers, and other stakeholders to develop guidelines, best practices, and regulatory frameworks that promote responsible and ethical use of these technologies. For example, organizations can establish ethical guidelines and principles for AI development, such as fairness, transparency, accountability, and societal impact, to guide the design, development, and deployment of AI-powered systems.

Furthermore, developers can adopt techniques such as fairness-aware machine learning, explainable AI, and algorithmic transparency to mitigate bias, enhance accountability, and promote transparency in AI-powered systems. For example, developers can use fairness-aware machine learning techniques to identify and mitigate biases in training data or algorithmic decisions, ensuring that AI-powered systems produce fair and equitable outcomes for all users.

Additionally, developers can promote transparency and accountability in AI-powered systems by providing explanations or justifications for algorithmic decisions, enabling users to understand how decisions are made and why certain outcomes are produced. For example, developers can use techniques such as model interpretability and explanation to provide insights into the inner workings of machine learning models and help users understand the factors influencing algorithmic decisions.

Moreover, developers can engage with stakeholders, including end-users, policymakers, and advocacy groups, to solicit feedback, address concerns, and build trust in AI-powered systems. By fostering open dialogue and collaboration, developers can ensure that AI and machine learning technologies are developed and deployed responsibly, ethically, and in the best interests of society.

In summary, understanding the potential impacts and ethical considerations of AI and machine learning is essential for developers, policymakers, and society to ensure responsible and ethical use of these technologies. While AI and machine learning offer tremendous potential to drive innovation and improve efficiency, they also raise significant ethical concerns related to privacy, bias, transparency, accountability, and societal impact that must be addressed to mitigate risks and promote responsible adoption of these technologies. By adopting ethical guidelines, promoting transparency and accountability, and engaging with stakeholders, developers can help ensure that AI and machine learning technologies are developed and deployed responsibly, ethically, and in the best interests of society.

BOOK 2
MASTERING AI PAIR PROGRAMMING
ADVANCED TECHNIQUES FOR DEVELOPERS

ROB BOTWRIGHT

Chapter 1: Advanced Concepts in AI Pair Programming

Neural network architectures are fundamental components of modern artificial intelligence and machine learning systems, playing a critical role in determining the capabilities, performance, and efficiency of these systems. A neural network architecture defines the structure, connectivity, and computational operations of a neural network, enabling it to learn from data, make predictions, and perform tasks ranging from image recognition and natural language processing to autonomous driving and drug discovery. By understanding the principles and characteristics of different neural network architectures, developers can design, train, and deploy neural networks effectively to solve a wide range of real-world problems.

One of the most common and widely used neural network architectures is the feedforward neural network, which consists of multiple layers of interconnected neurons organized in a sequential manner, with each neuron connected to neurons in the adjacent layers. Feedforward neural networks are typically used for supervised learning tasks such as classification and regression, where the network learns to map input data to output labels or values by adjusting the weights of connections between neurons during training. To deploy a feedforward neural network, developers can use libraries such as TensorFlow or PyTorch to define the network architecture, specify the training data, and optimize the network parameters using gradient descent-based optimization algorithms.

Another popular neural network architecture is the convolutional neural network (CNN), which is specifically designed for processing structured grid-like data such as images and video. CNNs leverage convolutional layers, pooling layers, and fully connected layers to learn hierarchical representations of input data, capturing spatial and temporal dependencies within the data. CNNs have achieved remarkable success in image recognition, object detection, and image segmentation tasks, surpassing human performance on various benchmark datasets. To deploy a CNN, developers can use pre-trained models available in deep learning libraries such as TensorFlow Hub or PyTorch Hub, fine-tune the models on domain-specific data, and evaluate their performance on task-specific metrics.

Recurrent neural networks (RNNs) are another important class of neural network architectures designed for processing sequential data such as time series, speech, and text. Unlike feedforward neural networks, which process input data in a single pass from input to output, RNNs have recurrent connections that allow them to maintain internal state and process sequences of variable length. This enables RNNs to model temporal dependencies and capture long-range dependencies in sequential data, making them well-suited for tasks such as speech recognition, language modeling, and machine translation. To deploy an RNN, developers can use libraries such as TensorFlow or PyTorch to define the network architecture, preprocess input sequences, and train the network using techniques such as backpropagation through time (BPTT).

Additionally, attention mechanisms have emerged as a powerful extension to traditional neural network architectures, enabling models to focus on relevant parts of input data and selectively attend to different aspects of the input during processing. Attention mechanisms have been widely adopted in natural language processing tasks such as machine translation, text summarization, and question answering, where they improve the performance of models by allowing them to attend to relevant words or phrases in the input text. To deploy models with attention mechanisms, developers can use libraries such as Hugging Face Transformers or TensorFlow Addons to incorporate attention layers into neural network architectures and fine-tune pre-trained models on task-specific data.

Furthermore, transformer architectures have revolutionized natural language processing and machine learning with their ability to model long-range dependencies and capture contextual information in large sequences of data. Transformer models, such as BERT, GPT, and T5, have achieved state-of-the-art performance on a wide range of natural language processing tasks, including language modeling, text classification, and question answering. To deploy transformer models, developers can use pre-trained models available in libraries such as Hugging Face Transformers or TensorFlow Hub, fine-tune the models on domain-specific data using transfer learning techniques, and evaluate their performance on task-specific benchmarks.

In addition to these commonly used neural network architectures, there are various specialized architectures designed for specific tasks or domains, such as graph neural networks for graph-structured data, capsule networks for image recognition, and generative adversarial networks (GANs) for generating realistic data samples. Each of these architectures has its own unique characteristics, advantages, and limitations, making them suitable for different types of problems and applications. By understanding the principles and capabilities of different neural network architectures, developers can select the most appropriate architecture for their specific use case, design efficient and effective models, and achieve state-of-the-art performance on their target tasks. Reinforcement learning (RL) techniques have gained significant attention in recent years for their ability to enable agents to learn optimal decision-making policies through interaction with an environment. RL is a subfield of machine learning that focuses on learning how to make sequential decisions to maximize cumulative rewards over time. Unlike supervised learning, where the model is trained on labeled data, and unsupervised learning, where the model learns patterns from unlabeled data, RL agents learn from feedback received from the environment in the form of rewards or penalties. By exploring various RL techniques, developers can build intelligent agents capable of autonomously learning to solve complex decision-making problems in domains such as robotics, gaming, finance, and healthcare.

One of the foundational concepts in RL is the Markov decision process (MDP), which provides a formal framework for modeling sequential decision-making problems. An MDP consists of a set of states, actions, transition probabilities, rewards, and a discount factor, where the agent interacts with the environment by selecting actions in states, receiving rewards, and transitioning to new states according to transition probabilities. To deploy an RL agent in an MDP, developers can use libraries such as OpenAI Gym or

TensorFlow Agents to define the environment, specify the agent's actions and rewards, and train the agent using RL algorithms such as Q-learning, SARSA, or Deep Q-Networks (DQN).

Q-learning is one of the simplest and most widely used RL algorithms for solving MDPs with discrete action spaces. In Q-learning, the agent learns a state-action value function (Q-function) that estimates the expected cumulative reward of taking a particular action in a given state. The agent updates its Q-values iteratively based on the observed rewards and transitions, using the Bellman equation to guide the learning process towards optimal policies. To implement Q-learning, developers can use Python and libraries such as NumPy to represent Q-values as tables or arrays, implement the Q-learning update rule, and train the agent by interacting with the environment and updating Q-values based on observed rewards and transitions.

Another popular RL algorithm is SARSA (State-Action-Reward-State-Action), which is similar to Q-learning but updates Q-values based on the observed next state and action rather than the maximum Q-value of the next state. SARSA is an on-policy RL algorithm, meaning that it learns the value of the policy being followed by the agent. To implement SARSA, developers can use similar techniques as Q-learning but update Q-values based on observed state-action-reward-state-action transitions, ensuring that the agent learns policies consistent with its current behavior.

Deep Q-Networks (DQN) are a class of RL algorithms that use deep neural networks to approximate the Q-function in high-dimensional state spaces, such as images or sensor data. DQN combines Q-learning with deep learning techniques to learn complex decision-making policies directly from raw input data, without the need for handcrafted features or domain-specific knowledge. To implement DQN, developers can use deep learning libraries such as TensorFlow or PyTorch to define the neural network architecture, preprocess input data, and train the network using gradient-based optimization algorithms such as stochastic gradient descent (SGD) or Adam.

Furthermore, policy gradient methods are a class of RL algorithms that directly learn the policy function, mapping states to actions, without explicitly estimating the value function. Policy gradient methods use gradient ascent to maximize the expected cumulative reward by adjusting the parameters of the policy network in the direction of higher rewards. To implement policy gradient methods, developers can use deep learning libraries such as TensorFlow or PyTorch to define the policy network architecture, specify the loss function as the expected cumulative reward, and train the network using gradient-based optimization algorithms.

Moreover, actor-critic methods combine elements of both value-based and policy-based RL approaches, leveraging separate actor and critic networks to learn the policy and value functions simultaneously. The actor network learns the policy function, mapping states to actions, while the critic network learns the value function, estimating the expected cumulative reward of following the policy. Actor-critic methods offer a balance between exploration and exploitation, enabling efficient and stable learning in continuous action spaces. To implement actor-critic methods, developers can use deep learning libraries such as TensorFlow or PyTorch to define the actor and critic network architectures, specify the loss functions for policy and value learning, and train the networks using gradient-based optimization algorithms.

In addition to these fundamental RL algorithms, there are various advanced techniques and extensions, such as deep deterministic policy gradients (DDPG), proximal policy optimization (PPO), and twin delayed deep deterministic policy gradients (TD3), that offer improved stability, sample efficiency, and performance for RL tasks. By exploring and experimenting with different RL techniques, developers can gain insights into their strengths and limitations, tailor them to specific problem domains, and build intelligent agents capable of learning complex decision-making policies in dynamic and uncertain environments.

Chapter 2: Deep Dive into Collaborative AI Development

Team dynamics play a crucial role in the success of AI pair programming initiatives, influencing collaboration, communication, and productivity among team members. AI pair programming involves developers working collaboratively with AI-powered tools to write, review, and maintain code, leveraging the strengths of both human expertise and machine intelligence to improve code quality and development efficiency. By understanding the dynamics of AI pair programming teams, organizations can foster a collaborative and supportive environment, facilitate knowledge sharing and skill development, and maximize the effectiveness of their AI pair programming efforts.

One aspect of team dynamics in AI pair programming is the distribution of roles and responsibilities among team members, including developers, AI specialists, and domain experts. Developers are responsible for writing and reviewing code, leveraging AI-powered tools to generate code snippets, refactor code, or debug issues. AI specialists play a crucial role in training and fine-tuning machine learning models, optimizing AI-powered tools for specific use cases, and providing technical support and guidance to developers. Domain experts contribute domain-specific knowledge and expertise, helping developers understand the context and requirements of the project and providing valuable insights and feedback on code quality and functionality.

To facilitate effective collaboration and communication among team members in AI pair programming teams, organizations can adopt various communication tools and platforms, such as Slack, Microsoft Teams, or Zoom, to facilitate real-time communication, instant messaging, and video conferencing. By providing a centralized platform for team communication and collaboration, organizations can ensure that team members can easily communicate, share ideas, and collaborate on code-related tasks, regardless of their physical location or time zone. Moreover, organizations can establish regular team meetings, stand-ups, or code review sessions to discuss project progress, address challenges, and provide feedback and support to team members.

Another aspect of team dynamics in AI pair programming is the establishment of a supportive and inclusive team culture that encourages collaboration, knowledge sharing, and continuous learning. Organizations can foster a culture of psychological safety, where team members feel comfortable expressing their ideas, asking questions, and seeking help without fear of judgment or criticism. By creating a supportive and inclusive environment, organizations can empower team members to share their knowledge and expertise, seek feedback and assistance from their peers, and collaborate effectively on code-related tasks. Additionally, organizations can encourage continuous learning and skill development by providing access to training resources, workshops, and educational opportunities related to AI pair programming techniques and tools.

In AI pair programming teams, effective leadership plays a crucial role in guiding the team, facilitating collaboration, and resolving conflicts or challenges that may arise during the development process. Team leaders can provide direction and guidance to team members, set clear goals and expectations for project outcomes, and allocate resources and responsibilities effectively to ensure that project milestones are met. Moreover, team leaders can act as advocates for AI pair programming within the organization, promoting its benefits, addressing concerns or objections, and facilitating the adoption of AI-powered tools and techniques among team members.

Furthermore, fostering a culture of experimentation and innovation can encourage team members to explore new ideas, techniques, and approaches to AI pair programming, driving continuous improvement and innovation in the development process. Organizations can create opportunities for team members to experiment with different AI-powered tools and techniques, conduct pilot projects or proof-of-concepts, and share their findings and insights with the rest of the team. By encouraging a culture of experimentation and innovation, organizations can empower team members to explore new ways of working, identify opportunities for improvement, and drive innovation in AI pair programming practices.

Moreover, effective conflict resolution and decision-making processes are essential for maintaining team cohesion and productivity in AI pair programming teams. Conflicts or disagreements may arise among team members due to differences in opinions, priorities, or approaches to problem-solving. To address conflicts constructively, organizations can establish clear guidelines and processes for resolving conflicts, such as open communication, active listening, and consensus-building techniques. By providing a structured framework for conflict resolution, organizations can ensure that conflicts are addressed in a timely and respectful manner, enabling team members to focus on their work and collaborate effectively towards project goals.

In summary, team dynamics play a crucial role in the success of AI pair programming initiatives, influencing collaboration, communication, and productivity among team members. By fostering a collaborative and supportive team culture, providing effective leadership and guidance, and promoting continuous learning and innovation, organizations can maximize the effectiveness of their AI pair programming efforts and drive success in their development projects. Through effective communication, collaboration, and conflict resolution processes, AI pair programming teams can harness the collective expertise and creativity of team members to develop high-quality software products and solutions efficiently and effectively.

Collaborative AI development relies heavily on a diverse array of tools and platforms designed to facilitate teamwork, streamline workflows, and maximize productivity among developers, data scientists, and other stakeholders involved in AI projects. These tools encompass a wide range of functionalities, including version control, project management, data visualization, model training, and deployment automation, catering to the unique requirements and challenges of AI development teams. By leveraging the right combination of tools and platforms, organizations can enhance collaboration, accelerate development cycles, and deliver innovative AI solutions to market more efficiently.

One of the foundational tools for collaborative AI development is version control systems, such as Git, which enable developers to track changes to source code, collaborate on codebases, and manage project repositories effectively. Git provides a distributed version control system that allows multiple developers to work on the same codebase simultaneously, enabling seamless collaboration and code sharing across teams. By using Git commands such as git clone, git pull, git push, and git merge, developers can clone repositories, synchronize changes with remote repositories, and merge code changes from different branches, ensuring consistency and integrity in collaborative development workflows.

GitHub is a popular platform built on top of Git, providing additional features and functionalities for collaborative software development, including issue tracking, pull requests, code reviews, and project management tools. GitHub enables developers to host, review, and manage code repositories, collaborate with team members, and coordinate development efforts efficiently. By leveraging GitHub's pull request workflow, developers can propose changes, request code reviews, and merge contributions from multiple collaborators seamlessly, fostering a culture of collaboration and code quality in AI development projects.

Another essential tool for collaborative AI development is integrated development environments (IDEs), such as PyCharm, Jupyter Notebook, and VS Code, which provide comprehensive coding environments with features such as code editing, debugging, and version control integration. IDEs offer a unified workspace for developers to write, test, and debug code, enabling seamless integration with version control systems and collaboration platforms. By using IDEs, developers can write Python scripts, analyze data, and train machine learning models in a unified environment, improving productivity and collaboration in AI development workflows.

Jupyter Notebook is particularly popular among data scientists and researchers for interactive data analysis and prototyping, allowing users to write and execute Python code in a web-based notebook interface. Jupyter Notebook supports the integration of code, text, and visualizations in a single document, enabling reproducible research and collaborative data exploration. By sharing Jupyter Notebooks through platforms such as GitHub or JupyterHub, data scientists can collaborate with team members, share insights, and iterate on analyses collaboratively, enhancing transparency and reproducibility in AI development projects.

Data visualization tools, such as Matplotlib, Seaborn, and Plotly, are essential for collaborative AI development, enabling developers and data scientists to explore and communicate insights from large datasets effectively. These tools provide a wide range of visualization techniques for analyzing and interpreting data, including scatter plots, histograms, and heatmaps, making it easier to identify patterns, trends, and outliers in complex datasets. By visualizing data using these tools, teams can gain deeper insights into data distributions, relationships, and trends, facilitating data-driven decision-making and collaboration in AI development projects.

Model training frameworks, such as TensorFlow, PyTorch, and scikit-learn, are fundamental tools for collaborative AI development, enabling developers and data scientists to build, train, and evaluate machine learning models efficiently. These frameworks provide a rich set of APIs and libraries for developing a wide range of AI applications, including deep learning, reinforcement learning, and classical machine learning. By using these frameworks, teams can experiment with different model architectures, training algorithms, and hyperparameters, iterate on model designs, and optimize model performance collaboratively, accelerating the development and deployment of AI solutions.

Moreover, cloud computing platforms, such as Amazon Web Services (AWS), Microsoft Azure, and Google Cloud Platform (GCP), offer a wide range of services and tools for collaborative AI development, including scalable compute resources, managed machine learning services, and data analytics tools. These platforms provide on-demand access to computing resources, storage, and infrastructure, enabling teams to deploy AI applications at scale, collaborate on data analysis and model training, and integrate AI capabilities into existing workflows seamlessly. By leveraging cloud computing platforms, organizations can reduce infrastructure costs, improve scalability and reliability, and accelerate time-to-market for AI solutions.

Furthermore, containerization and orchestration tools, such as Docker and Kubernetes, are essential for collaborative AI development, enabling teams to package, deploy, and manage AI applications consistently across different environments. Containers provide lightweight, portable runtime environments for applications and dependencies, ensuring consistency and reproducibility across development, testing, and production environments. By using Docker commands such as docker build, docker run, and docker push, teams can create container images, run containers locally or in the cloud, and share containerized applications with collaborators, streamlining deployment and collaboration in AI development workflows.

In addition to these tools and platforms, collaborative AI development also relies on effective project management tools, communication platforms, and knowledge sharing mechanisms to facilitate teamwork, coordination, and information exchange among team members. By leveraging a combination of tools and platforms tailored to the unique requirements and workflows of AI development teams, organizations can enhance collaboration, accelerate development cycles, and deliver innovative AI solutions to market more efficiently.

Chapter 3: Advanced Code Generation with AI Pair Programming

Code generation strategies for complex problems involve various techniques and approaches aimed at automating the process of writing code to solve intricate programming challenges. These strategies encompass a range of methodologies, tools, and best practices designed to streamline development workflows, improve code quality, and enhance productivity when tackling complex problems in software development. By employing effective code generation strategies, developers can simplify the implementation of complex algorithms, reduce the risk of errors, and accelerate the delivery of robust and scalable solutions to challenging problems.

One common approach to code generation for complex problems is the use of code templates or scaffolding tools, which provide pre-defined structures or patterns for implementing common programming tasks or design patterns. These templates serve as starting points for developers, allowing them to quickly generate boilerplate code for specific functionalities or components, such as data structures, algorithms, or user interface elements. By using templates, developers can avoid repetitive coding tasks, adhere to established coding conventions, and focus on solving the unique aspects of the problem at hand. Popular scaffolding tools include Yeoman, which generates project scaffolds for web applications, and Cookiecutter, which creates project templates for Python-based projects.

Another approach to code generation for complex problems is the use of code synthesis techniques, which involve automatically generating code from high-level specifications or domain-specific languages (DSLs). Code synthesis tools analyze input specifications or requirements and generate corresponding code that meets the specified criteria, such as performance constraints, resource usage, or architectural constraints. These tools can be particularly useful for generating code for domain-specific tasks or applications, where manual coding may be error-prone or time-consuming. For example, Rosetta, a code synthesis tool developed by Microsoft Research, automatically generates efficient implementations of sorting algorithms from high-level specifications.

Furthermore, domain-specific code generators are specialized tools that translate domain-specific models or descriptions into executable code tailored to specific problem domains or application contexts. These generators typically operate at a higher level of abstraction than traditional programming languages, allowing developers to express complex concepts and relationships in a more intuitive and concise manner. Domain-specific code generators are commonly used in fields such as scientific computing, embedded systems, and financial modeling, where the complexity of the problem domain warrants specialized tools and techniques. For instance, Simulink, a graphical modeling environment developed by MathWorks, enables engineers to model and simulate complex dynamical systems using block diagrams, which are automatically translated into executable code for real-time control and simulation.

Moreover, meta-programming techniques, such as code generation through reflection or template metaprogramming, enable developers to generate code dynamically at runtime or compile time based on runtime information or compile-time parameters. These techniques allow developers to write code that generates or manipulates other code, enabling advanced code generation and customization capabilities. For example, in languages such as C++ and Java, developers can use template metaprogramming to write generic code that operates on types, enabling code generation and optimization at compile time based on type information.

Additionally, model-driven development (MDD) is an approach to software development that emphasizes the use of models as primary artifacts for designing, implementing, and evolving software systems. In MDD, developers create abstract models of the system under development using modeling languages such as UML (Unified Modeling Language) or DSLs tailored to specific problem domains. These models capture the essential aspects of the system's structure, behavior, and functionality, which can then be automatically transformed into executable code using code generation tools or model compilers. By leveraging MDD techniques, developers can reduce the complexity of software development, improve abstraction and modularity, and enhance the maintainability and scalability of software systems.

Furthermore, code generation frameworks and libraries provide developers with reusable components and utilities for generating code programmatically, enabling the automation of common coding tasks and patterns. These frameworks abstract away low-level details of code generation, providing high-level APIs and abstractions for defining code templates, generating code from models or specifications, and customizing code generation behavior. For example, Java Annotation Processing Tool (APT) and Java Compiler API provide facilities for generating code dynamically during the compilation process based on annotations or metadata embedded in source code.

In summary, code generation strategies for complex problems encompass a range of techniques, tools, and approaches aimed at automating the process of writing code to solve intricate programming challenges. By employing effective code generation strategies, developers can streamline development workflows, improve code quality, and enhance productivity when tackling complex problems in software development. Whether through the use of code templates, synthesis techniques, domain-specific code generators, or meta-programming techniques, code generation offers valuable opportunities for simplifying coding tasks, reducing errors, and accelerating the delivery of robust and scalable solutions to challenging problems.

Handling edge cases and exceptions is an essential aspect of software development, requiring careful consideration and robust strategies to ensure the reliability, stability, and resilience of software systems in real-world scenarios. Edge cases refer to unusual or unexpected inputs, conditions, or scenarios that fall outside the typical range of operation or behavior of a software application. These edge cases may arise due to rare conditions, boundary conditions, or exceptional circumstances that developers may not have anticipated during the design and implementation phase of a software project. Exception handling, on the other hand, involves identifying, managing, and gracefully recovering from errors, faults, or exceptional conditions that occur during the execution of a software program, ensuring that the application can continue to operate correctly and safely in the presence of unexpected events or failures.

One common approach to handling edge cases and exceptions is to perform thorough testing and validation of software systems under a wide range of input conditions, including both typical and atypical scenarios. Software testing techniques, such as unit testing, integration testing, and system testing, enable developers to identify and address edge cases and exceptional conditions early in the development process, reducing the likelihood of encountering unexpected behavior or errors in production environments. By designing comprehensive test suites that cover a diverse set of input values, boundary conditions, and error scenarios, developers can uncover potential issues, validate the correctness of the software implementation, and improve the overall quality and reliability of the software product.

Moreover, defensive programming practices involve anticipating and guarding against potential edge cases and exceptional conditions by incorporating error handling mechanisms, validation checks, and fail-safe mechanisms into the software code. Defensive programming techniques, such as input validation, range checking, and boundary testing, help detect and mitigate potential issues related to edge cases and exceptional conditions before they manifest as errors or failures in the software application. By proactively addressing potential risks and vulnerabilities, developers can improve the robustness, stability, and security of the software system, reducing the likelihood of unexpected behavior or system failures in production environments.

Furthermore, error handling mechanisms, such as try-catch blocks, exception handling, and error recovery strategies, enable developers to detect, handle, and recover from exceptional conditions or errors gracefully during the execution of a software program. In languages such as Java, C#, and Python, developers can use try-catch blocks to encapsulate code segments that may raise exceptions or errors, allowing them to catch and handle specific types of exceptions, log error messages, and execute error recovery logic as needed. By implementing robust error handling mechanisms, developers can prevent unexpected program terminations, provide meaningful error messages to users, and maintain the overall stability and reliability of the software application.

Additionally, logging and monitoring tools provide valuable insights into the behavior and performance of software systems, enabling developers to track and analyze edge cases, exceptions, and error conditions in real-time. Logging frameworks, such as Log4j, Serilog, and Winston, allow developers to record diagnostic information, error messages, and stack traces during the execution of a software program, facilitating troubleshooting, debugging, and root cause analysis of issues related to edge cases and exceptional conditions. By monitoring application logs and performance metrics using tools such as Prometheus, Grafana, or ELK Stack, developers can identify patterns, trends, and anomalies indicative of edge cases or exceptional behavior, enabling proactive intervention and remediation of potential issues before they impact system performance or user experience.

Moreover, fault tolerance and resilience engineering principles focus on designing software systems that can continue to operate correctly and reliably in the presence of faults, errors, or exceptional conditions. Techniques such as redundancy, graceful degradation, and fault isolation enable developers to build resilient systems that can withstand failures and recover gracefully from unexpected events or conditions. By designing systems with built-in mechanisms for fault detection, isolation, and recovery, developers can minimize the impact of edge cases and exceptions on system availability, performance, and reliability, ensuring uninterrupted operation and continuity of service for users.

In summary, handling edge cases and exceptions is a critical aspect of software development, requiring developers to employ robust strategies, techniques, and mechanisms to ensure the reliability, stability, and resilience of software systems in real-world scenarios. By performing thorough testing, incorporating defensive programming practices, implementing robust error handling mechanisms, and leveraging logging and monitoring tools, developers can identify, manage, and recover from edge cases and exceptional conditions effectively, mitigating the risk of unexpected behavior or failures in production environments. Additionally, by embracing fault tolerance and resilience engineering principles, developers can design software systems that can withstand faults, errors, and exceptional conditions, ensuring uninterrupted operation and continuity of service for users under diverse and challenging conditions.

Chapter 4: Handling Complex Projects with AI Pair Programming

Project management strategies for AI pair programming involve a set of methodologies, practices, and techniques aimed at effectively organizing, coordinating, and overseeing collaborative development efforts between human developers and AI assistants. In AI pair programming, developers work closely with AI tools, such as GitHub Copilot, to collaboratively write, review, and debug code, leveraging the strengths of both human creativity and machine intelligence to improve productivity, code quality, and development outcomes. Effective project management in AI pair programming requires careful planning, communication, and coordination to ensure that development tasks are completed efficiently, deadlines are met, and project goals are achieved. By adopting appropriate project management strategies and tools, teams can harness the full potential of AI pair programming to deliver high-quality software solutions effectively and efficiently.

One essential project management strategy for AI pair programming is agile development, which emphasizes iterative, incremental, and collaborative approaches to software development. Agile methodologies, such as Scrum, Kanban, and Extreme Programming (XP), provide frameworks for organizing development work into short, time-boxed iterations or sprints, during which teams plan, execute, and review development tasks collaboratively. By adopting agile practices such as daily stand-up meetings, sprint planning sessions, and retrospective meetings, AI pair programming teams can maintain transparency, adaptability, and accountability throughout the development process, ensuring that project priorities are aligned, risks are managed, and progress is monitored effectively.

Furthermore, effective communication and collaboration are essential for successful AI pair programming projects. Teams should establish clear channels of communication, such as Slack channels, Microsoft Teams, or Discord servers, where developers can discuss ideas, share updates, and coordinate development activities in real-time. Additionally, regular meetings, such as pair programming sessions, code reviews, and sprint demos, provide opportunities for developers to collaborate, exchange feedback, and align on project goals and priorities. By fostering a culture of open communication, collaboration, and knowledge sharing, AI pair programming teams can leverage the collective expertise and creativity of team members to solve complex problems and deliver high-quality software solutions.

Moreover, task management tools, such as Jira, Trello, or Asana, play a crucial role in organizing and prioritizing development tasks, tracking progress, and managing project timelines in AI pair programming projects. These tools enable teams to create, assign, and track tasks, set deadlines, and visualize project workflows using boards, cards, or tickets. By breaking down project tasks into smaller, manageable units and assigning them to individual team members, project managers can ensure that development work is distributed evenly, dependencies are managed effectively, and progress is tracked transparently. Additionally, by integrating task management tools with version control systems such as GitHub or GitLab, teams can link code changes to specific tasks or issues, facilitating traceability and accountability in the development process.

Furthermore, continuous integration and continuous delivery (CI/CD) practices enable AI pair programming teams to automate the process of building, testing, and deploying software changes rapidly and reliably. CI/CD pipelines, configured using tools such as Jenkins, CircleCI, or GitHub Actions, automate repetitive tasks such as code compilation, unit testing, code analysis, and deployment, enabling teams to deliver new features and updates to production environments with minimal manual intervention. By automating the software delivery process, AI pair programming teams can reduce the risk of errors, improve the speed of delivery, and ensure that code changes are tested and validated consistently across different environments, enhancing the overall quality and reliability of the software product.

Moreover, version control systems, such as Git, are essential for managing code changes, tracking revisions, and facilitating collaboration in AI pair programming projects. Version control systems enable developers to work on code changes concurrently, track changes to source code, and merge contributions from multiple team members seamlessly. By using Git commands such as git clone, git pull, git push, and git merge, developers can clone repositories, synchronize changes with remote repositories, and resolve merge conflicts efficiently, ensuring that code changes are integrated and deployed smoothly. Additionally, by leveraging branching and tagging mechanisms, teams can manage feature branches, release branches, and version tags effectively, enabling parallel development and release management in AI pair programming projects.

In summary, effective project management strategies are essential for orchestrating collaborative development efforts in AI pair programming projects. By adopting agile methodologies, fostering communication and collaboration, leveraging task management tools, automating software delivery pipelines, and utilizing version control systems, teams can streamline development workflows, improve productivity, and deliver high-quality software solutions efficiently and effectively. By embracing these project management strategies and tools, AI pair programming teams can unlock the full potential of human-AI collaboration, enabling them to tackle complex problems, innovate rapidly, and deliver value to stakeholders with confidence and agility.

In software development, finding the right balance between flexibility and rigidity in project structures is crucial for ensuring project success. Project structures define the organization, hierarchy, and workflow of development tasks, and striking a balance between flexibility and rigidity requires careful consideration of project requirements, team dynamics, and organizational constraints. Flexibility allows for adaptability to changing requirements, rapid iteration, and innovation, while rigidity provides stability, consistency, and predictability in project execution. Achieving an optimal balance between these two contrasting attributes requires a nuanced approach that combines elements of both flexibility and rigidity to meet the diverse needs of software development projects.

One way to balance flexibility and rigidity in project structures is through the adoption of agile methodologies, such as Scrum or Kanban. Agile methodologies advocate for iterative, incremental development cycles that prioritize flexibility, adaptability, and customer collaboration. In Scrum, for example, development work is organized into short, time-boxed iterations called sprints, during which cross-functional teams collaborate to deliver potentially shippable increments of software. While Scrum provides a flexible framework that allows teams to adjust priorities and respond to changing requirements, it also imposes certain rigidity through fixed sprint durations, defined roles, and ceremonies such as sprint planning, daily stand-ups, and sprint reviews.

Moreover, establishing clear project goals, milestones, and deliverables can help strike a balance between flexibility and rigidity in project structures. By defining clear objectives and success criteria upfront, teams can maintain focus, alignment, and accountability throughout the project lifecycle. Project management tools such as Jira, Trello, or Asana can be used to create project roadmaps, define tasks, and track progress towards milestones. While these tools provide flexibility in task management and prioritization, they also introduce a level of rigidity through predefined workflows, status categories, and progress tracking mechanisms.

Additionally, creating modular and scalable project architectures can facilitate flexibility while mitigating the risks associated with rigidity in software development projects. Modular architectures, such as microservices or component-based architectures, allow for the independent development, deployment, and scaling of discrete components or services within a larger system. By decoupling dependencies and defining clear interfaces between components, teams can achieve flexibility in development, testing, and deployment while maintaining a level of rigidity in the overall system structure. Version control systems such as Git enable teams to manage changes to codebases, track revisions, and enforce coding standards, providing a structured approach to collaboration while allowing for flexibility in code organization and evolution.

Furthermore, fostering a culture of experimentation, innovation, and continuous improvement can help balance flexibility and rigidity in project structures. Encouraging team members to explore new ideas, technologies, and approaches fosters creativity and agility while providing opportunities to learn from successes and failures. Techniques such as rapid prototyping, A/B testing, and continuous integration enable teams to validate hypotheses, gather feedback, and iterate quickly on product features and designs. While experimentation introduces a degree of uncertainty and risk, it also drives innovation and drives continuous improvement, striking a balance between flexibility and rigidity in project structures.

Moreover, implementing effective change management processes can help mitigate the risks associated with introducing flexibility into project structures. Change management practices, such as impact assessment, stakeholder engagement, and communication planning, enable teams to evaluate the potential impact of changes, solicit feedback from stakeholders, and communicate changes effectively to minimize disruption. Configuration management tools such as Ansible, Puppet, or Chef can be used to automate the deployment and configuration of software environments, ensuring consistency and repeatability while allowing for flexibility in infrastructure provisioning and management.

Additionally, fostering cross-functional collaboration and knowledge sharing can enhance flexibility while reducing the negative effects of rigidity in project structures. By breaking down silos between teams and departments, organizations can leverage the diverse skills, perspectives, and expertise of team members to tackle complex problems and drive innovation. Techniques such as pair programming, code reviews, and collaborative design sessions enable teams to share knowledge, review code, and make informed decisions collaboratively, fostering a culture of collective ownership and continuous learning. While collaboration introduces a degree of coordination overhead, it also promotes resilience, adaptability, and creativity in project execution.

In summary, balancing flexibility and rigidity in project structures is essential for achieving success in software development projects. By adopting agile methodologies, defining clear project goals and milestones, creating modular and scalable architectures, fostering a culture of experimentation and continuous improvement, implementing effective change management processes, and promoting cross-functional collaboration, teams can strike an optimal balance between flexibility and rigidity, enabling them to adapt to changing requirements, innovate rapidly, and deliver high-quality software solutions efficiently and effectively.

Chapter 5: Maximizing Efficiency in AI Pair Programming Sessions

Effective time management is crucial for successful pair programming, a collaborative development practice where two programmers work together on the same codebase. Pair programming offers numerous benefits, including improved code quality, faster issue resolution, and knowledge sharing, but it also requires careful planning and coordination to ensure productivity and efficiency. By employing various time management techniques, pair programming teams can optimize their workflow, minimize distractions, and maximize the value they deliver. From setting clear goals and priorities to leveraging productivity tools and techniques, there are several strategies that pair programmers can use to manage their time effectively and make the most out of their collaborative coding sessions.

One fundamental time management technique for effective pair programming is setting clear goals and objectives for each coding session. Before starting a pair programming session, team members should discuss and agree on the specific tasks or features they intend to work on, as well as the desired outcomes or deliverables. By setting clear goals and priorities, pair programmers can focus their efforts on the most important tasks, avoid unnecessary distractions, and ensure that they make meaningful progress during the session. Tools such as Jira, Trello, or Asana can be used to create task lists, assign priorities, and track progress towards goals, helping teams stay organized and focused on their objectives.

Moreover, timeboxing is a useful technique for managing time during pair programming sessions. Timeboxing involves allocating a fixed amount of time to work on a specific task or activity, after which the team evaluates progress and decides whether to continue or switch to another task. By breaking down coding sessions into shorter, focused time intervals, pair programmers can maintain momentum, avoid burnout, and ensure that they make steady progress towards their goals. Tools such as Pomodoro timers or time tracking apps can help teams implement timeboxing effectively, providing reminders and alerts to signal when it's time to take breaks or switch tasks.

Furthermore, effective communication and collaboration are essential for managing time during pair programming sessions. Team members should establish clear communication channels, such as video calls, chat platforms, or screen-sharing tools, to facilitate real-time collaboration and information sharing. During coding sessions, pair programmers should communicate openly, ask questions, and provide feedback to each other to ensure that they stay aligned and focused on the task at hand. Techniques such as active listening, paraphrasing, and summarizing can help pair programmers clarify misunderstandings, resolve issues, and make decisions efficiently, saving time and avoiding unnecessary delays.

Additionally, leveraging code review practices can help pair programmers identify and address issues early in the development process, reducing the time spent on debugging and troubleshooting later on. By reviewing each other's code during pair programming sessions, team members can spot potential errors, inconsistencies, or inefficiencies and provide constructive feedback to improve code quality and maintainability. Tools such as GitHub, Bitbucket, or GitLab offer built-in code review features that enable teams to create, review, and merge code changes collaboratively, streamlining the review process and ensuring that code changes are thoroughly evaluated before being integrated into the codebase.

Moreover, automation tools and techniques can help pair programmers streamline repetitive tasks and eliminate manual overhead, freeing up time for more productive activities. By automating common development tasks such as code formatting, testing, and deployment, teams can reduce the time spent on manual labor and focus their efforts on higher-value activities such as problem-solving and innovation. Continuous integration and continuous delivery (CI/CD) pipelines, configured using tools such as Jenkins, CircleCI, or GitHub Actions, automate the process of building, testing, and deploying code changes, enabling teams to deliver new features and updates to production environments quickly and reliably.

Additionally, prioritizing tasks based on their impact and urgency can help pair programmers allocate their time and resources effectively, ensuring that they address the most critical issues first and avoid getting bogged down by less important tasks. Techniques such as the Eisenhower Matrix or the MoSCoW method can help teams prioritize tasks based on their importance and urgency, allowing them to focus on high-priority items while deferring or delegating lower-priority tasks as needed. By aligning their efforts with project goals and stakeholder expectations, pair programmers can ensure that they deliver maximum value with the time and resources available to them.

In summary, effective time management is essential for successful pair programming, enabling teams to collaborate efficiently, stay focused on their goals, and deliver high-quality software solutions. By setting clear goals and priorities, leveraging timeboxing techniques, communicating effectively, conducting code reviews, automating repetitive tasks, and prioritizing tasks based on impact and urgency, pair programmers can optimize their workflow, minimize distractions, and maximize the value they deliver. By adopting these time management techniques and practices, pair programming teams can achieve greater productivity, efficiency, and satisfaction in their collaborative coding efforts.

Effective communication is paramount in any collaborative endeavor, including software development. Optimizing communication channels for efficiency involves selecting and utilizing the most suitable tools and methods to facilitate clear, timely, and productive interactions among team members. In today's fast-paced development environments, where teams are often distributed across different locations and time zones, choosing the right communication channels can significantly impact productivity, collaboration, and project outcomes. By considering factors such as team preferences, project requirements, and communication goals, teams can optimize their communication channels to ensure seamless information exchange, decision-making, and problem-solving.

One fundamental aspect of optimizing communication channels for efficiency is selecting the appropriate tools and platforms that best suit the needs and preferences of the team. There is a wide range of communication tools available, including email, instant messaging apps, video conferencing platforms, and project management software, each offering distinct features and capabilities. Teams should evaluate their communication requirements, such as real-time messaging, file sharing, or video conferencing, and choose tools that align with their workflow and collaboration style. Popular communication tools such as Slack, Microsoft Teams, or Discord offer integrated messaging, file sharing, and collaboration features, allowing teams to communicate effectively and stay connected regardless of their physical location.

Moreover, establishing clear guidelines and protocols for communication can help streamline interactions and avoid misunderstandings or delays. Teams should define communication norms, such as response times, availability hours, and preferred channels for different types of communication, to ensure consistency and clarity in their interactions. For example, teams may set expectations for responding to messages within a certain timeframe or use specific channels for urgent or time-sensitive communications. By establishing clear communication protocols, teams can minimize ambiguity, reduce the risk of miscommunication, and ensure that important information reaches the intended recipients promptly.

Additionally, leveraging asynchronous communication methods can enhance efficiency and flexibility, particularly for distributed teams or those working across different time zones. Asynchronous communication allows team members to exchange messages, share updates, and collaborate on tasks without requiring real-time interaction. Email, project management software, and asynchronous messaging apps such as Slack or Microsoft

Teams offer features such as threads, channels, and notifications, enabling teams to communicate asynchronously while maintaining context and continuity. By embracing asynchronous communication, teams can accommodate diverse schedules, reduce dependencies on simultaneous availability, and foster productivity and collaboration across geographically dispersed teams.

Furthermore, integrating communication tools with other development tools and workflows can streamline information exchange and decision-making in software development projects. Many communication platforms offer integrations with project management, version control, and issue tracking tools, allowing teams to access relevant information and collaborate seamlessly within their preferred communication channels. For example, tools such as Slack or Microsoft Teams can be integrated with project management platforms like Jira or Trello, enabling teams to receive notifications, create tasks, and share updates directly from their communication channels. By integrating communication tools with other development workflows, teams can eliminate context switching, reduce cognitive load, and improve productivity by centralizing information and activities within a single interface.

Moreover, promoting a culture of open communication, transparency, and feedback can foster trust and collaboration among team members, leading to more effective communication and better project outcomes. Teams should encourage regular check-ins, status updates, and team meetings to share progress, discuss challenges, and align on priorities. Additionally, fostering a culture of constructive feedback and active listening can encourage team members to voice their ideas, concerns, and suggestions openly, facilitating better problem-solving and decision-making. By creating a supportive and inclusive communication environment, teams can strengthen relationships, build rapport, and enhance collaboration, ultimately improving efficiency and performance.

In summary, optimizing communication channels for efficiency is essential for successful software development projects. By selecting the right tools, establishing clear guidelines and protocols, leveraging asynchronous communication methods, integrating communication tools with other development workflows, and promoting a culture of open communication and feedback, teams can enhance productivity, collaboration, and project outcomes. Effective communication channels enable teams to exchange information, make decisions, and solve problems efficiently, ultimately contributing to the success and satisfaction of both team members and stakeholders.

Chapter 6: Fine-Tuning AI Models for Pair Programming

Hyperparameter optimization is a critical aspect of machine learning model development, involving the search for the optimal set of hyperparameters that maximize model performance. Hyperparameters are parameters that govern the behavior of machine learning algorithms and models, such as learning rates, regularization strengths, and network architectures. The selection of appropriate hyperparameters significantly impacts the performance, accuracy, and generalization ability of machine learning models. However, finding the optimal hyperparameters can be a challenging and time-consuming task due to the large search space and the complex interactions between hyperparameters. To address this challenge, various hyperparameter optimization techniques have been developed, ranging from manual tuning to automated optimization algorithms. By leveraging these techniques, data scientists and machine learning practitioners can efficiently explore the hyperparameter space, identify promising configurations, and improve the performance of their machine learning models.

One common approach to hyperparameter optimization is manual tuning, where data scientists manually adjust hyperparameters based on intuition, domain knowledge, and experimentation. In this approach, data scientists typically start with default hyperparameter values and iteratively modify them based on model performance on a validation dataset. For example, in a neural network model, data scientists may adjust parameters such as learning rates, batch sizes, and dropout rates to improve model accuracy and convergence. While manual tuning provides flexibility and control over hyperparameter selection, it can be time-consuming, subjective, and prone to human bias. Moreover, manual tuning may not effectively explore the entire hyperparameter space, leading to suboptimal model performance.

Another approach to hyperparameter optimization is grid search, a systematic technique that evaluates model performance across a predefined grid of hyperparameter values. In grid search, data scientists specify a set of hyperparameter values for each hyperparameter of interest, and the algorithm exhaustively evaluates all possible combinations of these values using cross-validation. For example, in a support vector machine (SVM) model, data scientists may specify a grid of values for parameters such as the kernel type, regularization strength, and gamma value. Grid search then trains and evaluates the model for each combination of hyperparameter values and selects the configuration with the highest performance. While grid search is simple to implement and interpretable, it suffers from high computational costs, especially when the hyperparameter space is large or when the model training process is computationally intensive.

A more efficient alternative to grid search is random search, which samples hyperparameter values randomly from predefined distributions and evaluates model performance for each sampled configuration. Unlike grid search, random search does not require exhaustive evaluation of all possible hyperparameter combinations, making it more computationally efficient, especially for high-dimensional hyperparameter spaces. Additionally, random search tends to explore a broader range of hyperparameter values, potentially leading to better model performance compared to grid search. However, random search may still suffer from suboptimal exploration of the hyperparameter space, particularly when the distributions of hyperparameters are not well-understood or when certain hyperparameters have a significant impact on model performance.

A more sophisticated approach to hyperparameter optimization is Bayesian optimization, a probabilistic optimization technique that uses Bayesian inference to model the relationship between hyperparameters and model performance. Bayesian optimization maintains a probabilistic surrogate model of the objective function (i.e., model performance) and iteratively selects hyperparameter configurations to evaluate based on an acquisition function that balances exploration and exploitation. By leveraging information from previous evaluations, Bayesian optimization can efficiently navigate the hyperparameter space and identify promising configurations with minimal evaluations. Popular implementations of Bayesian optimization include the Tree-structured Parzen Estimator (TPE) and the Gaussian Process-based Bayesian optimization. While Bayesian optimization tends to outperform random search and grid search in terms of convergence speed and sample efficiency, it requires careful tuning of hyperparameters such as the acquisition function and surrogate model, as well as computational resources for model fitting and evaluation.

Furthermore, evolutionary algorithms, inspired by biological evolution, can be applied to hyperparameter optimization by treating hyperparameter configurations as individuals in a population and iteratively evolving better solutions over generations. Genetic algorithms, particle swarm optimization, and differential evolution are examples of evolutionary algorithms that have been adapted for hyperparameter optimization. In these algorithms, hyperparameter configurations are represented as chromosomes or particles, and genetic operators such as mutation, crossover, and selection are used to generate new configurations based on the performance of existing ones. While evolutionary algorithms can effectively explore complex, multimodal hyperparameter spaces and escape local optima, they may suffer from high computational costs, especially for large-scale or high-dimensional optimization problems.

Moreover, meta-learning approaches, such as model-based reinforcement learning and meta-learning from data, have been proposed for hyperparameter optimization. In model-based reinforcement learning, an agent learns to select hyperparameter configurations by interacting with an environment that simulates model training and evaluation. The agent receives feedback on the performance of each configuration and updates its policy based on past experiences to improve future selections. In meta-learning from data, meta-features extracted from the dataset or model architecture are used to train meta-learners that predict the performance of different hyperparameter configurations. By leveraging meta-features and meta-learners, meta-learning approaches can generalize across datasets and model architectures and accelerate the hyperparameter optimization process. However, meta-learning approaches may require significant computational resources for training meta-learners and simulating model training, and their performance may depend on the quality and representativeness of the training data.

In summary, hyperparameter optimization is a critical aspect of machine learning model development, enabling data scientists and machine learning practitioners to identify optimal hyperparameter configurations that maximize model performance. Various techniques, ranging from manual tuning to automated optimization algorithms such as grid search, random search, Bayesian optimization, evolutionary algorithms, and meta-learning approaches, have been proposed for hyperparameter optimization. Each technique has its strengths and limitations in terms of computational efficiency, sample efficiency, and generalization ability, and the choice of technique depends on factors such as the size of the hyperparameter space, computational resources, and optimization objectives. By leveraging these techniques, data scientists can effectively explore the hyperparameter space, identify promising configurations, and improve the performance of their machine learning models.

Model interpretability and debugging are essential aspects of machine learning model development, enabling data scientists and machine learning practitioners to understand, interpret, and diagnose the behavior of their models. In today's complex machine learning landscape, where models are increasingly deployed in real-world applications with significant implications for decision-making and human welfare, understanding how models make predictions and identifying potential sources of errors or biases is crucial for ensuring model reliability, fairness, and accountability. Model interpretability refers to the ability to explain the predictions and decisions of machine learning models in a human-understandable and interpretable manner, while model debugging involves identifying and diagnosing issues or errors in model behavior, such as incorrect predictions, biases, or data quality issues. By employing various techniques and tools for model interpretability and debugging, data scientists can gain insights into model behavior, detect potential issues early in the development process, and build more reliable and trustworthy machine learning systems.

One common approach to model interpretability is feature importance analysis, which aims to identify the most influential features or variables in a machine learning model's predictions. Feature importance analysis techniques such as permutation feature importance, SHAP (SHapley Additive exPlanations), and

LIME (Local Interpretable Model-agnostic Explanations) can help data scientists understand which features contribute most to a model's predictions and how they influence the model's output. For example, in a classification task, feature importance analysis can reveal which input features are most indicative of different classes or outcomes, helping data scientists identify relevant factors driving model predictions. By visualizing feature importance scores or generating feature importance plots, data scientists can communicate the relative importance of different features to stakeholders and domain experts, facilitating model interpretation and decision-making.

Moreover, model interpretability techniques such as partial dependence plots and individual conditional expectation (ICE) plots provide insights into how individual features affect model predictions and how their effects vary across different input values. Partial dependence plots visualize the relationship between a target feature and the model's predictions while marginalizing over the values of other features, allowing data scientists to examine the average effect of a feature on model predictions. ICE plots, on the other hand, show the predictions of the model for individual instances as the value of a target feature varies, enabling data scientists to explore how the model's predictions change for different input values. By analyzing partial dependence plots and ICE plots, data scientists can identify nonlinear relationships between features and predictions, detect potential model biases or inconsistencies, and gain a deeper understanding of the underlying patterns captured by the model.

Additionally, surrogate models and global surrogate models provide alternative representations of complex machine learning models in simpler, interpretable forms. Surrogate models, such as decision trees or linear models, are trained to approximate the predictions of a black-box model using interpretable features, making it easier for data scientists to understand how the black-box model makes predictions. Global surrogate models aim to capture the overall behavior of the black-box model across the entire input space, providing insights into its decision-making process and internal logic. By comparing the predictions of the surrogate model with those of the black-box model, data scientists can validate the fidelity of the surrogate model and identify potential discrepancies or biases in the black-box model's predictions. Surrogate models and global surrogate models offer a transparent and interpretable way to understand complex machine learning models, making them valuable tools for model interpretability and debugging.

Furthermore, local explanation techniques such as counterfactual explanations and adversarial attacks can help data scientists understand how individual predictions are generated by machine learning models and identify potential vulnerabilities or weaknesses in model behavior. Counterfactual explanations provide interpretable explanations for individual predictions by generating hypothetical instances that, when fed into the model, result in a different prediction outcome. By analyzing counterfactual explanations, data scientists can understand the decision boundaries of the model, identify regions of input space where the model's predictions are uncertain or inconsistent, and diagnose potential sources of errors or biases. Adversarial attacks, on the other hand, aim to manipulate model predictions by perturbing input instances in imperceptible ways to force the model to make incorrect predictions. By probing the robustness and reliability of machine learning models through adversarial attacks, data scientists can uncover vulnerabilities, biases, and limitations in model behavior and develop more robust and trustworthy models.

Moreover, model debugging techniques such as residual analysis, error analysis, and sensitivity analysis can help data scientists diagnose issues or errors in model behavior and identify opportunities for improvement. Residual analysis involves examining the differences between the observed outcomes and the model predictions to identify patterns or trends that may indicate systematic errors or biases in the model. Error analysis focuses on analyzing the types and causes of prediction errors made by the model, such as misclassifications or mispredictions, to understand the root causes of model performance issues. Sensitivity analysis investigates how changes in input features or model parameters affect model predictions and performance, enabling data scientists to assess the robustness and stability of the model under different conditions. By conducting thorough model debugging and analysis, data scientists can identify potential sources of errors or biases, refine model performance, and build more reliable and accurate machine learning systems.

In summary, model interpretability and debugging are essential aspects of machine learning model development, enabling data scientists and machine learning practitioners to understand, interpret, and diagnose the behavior of their models. By employing various techniques such as feature importance analysis, partial dependence plots, surrogate models, local explanation techniques, and model debugging techniques, data scientists can gain insights into model behavior, detect potential issues or biases, and build more reliable and trustworthy machine learning systems. Model interpretability and debugging techniques play a crucial role in ensuring the transparency, fairness, and accountability of machine learning models and are essential for building responsible and ethical AI systems.

Chapter 7: Addressing Challenges in AI Pair Programming

Addressing bias and class imbalance is paramount in building fair, reliable, and effective AI models that can be deployed responsibly in various real-world applications. Bias refers to systematic errors or prejudices in the data or model that lead to unfair or discriminatory outcomes, while class imbalance occurs when the distribution of classes in the dataset is uneven, resulting in poor performance for minority classes. Bias and class imbalance can significantly impact the performance, accuracy, and fairness of AI models, leading to skewed predictions, unequal treatment, and perpetuation of societal inequalities. Overcoming bias and imbalance in AI models requires a multifaceted approach that involves data preprocessing, model selection, and post-processing techniques to mitigate bias, address class imbalance, and promote fairness, transparency, and accountability in AI systems.

One common approach to overcoming bias in AI models is data preprocessing, which involves identifying and mitigating biases in the training data before model training. Data preprocessing techniques such as data augmentation, data cleaning, and data rebalancing can help reduce bias and improve the representativeness and diversity of the training data. For example, data augmentation techniques such as oversampling or undersampling can be used to balance the distribution of classes in the dataset, ensuring that minority classes are adequately represented during model training. Additionally, data cleaning techniques such as outlier detection or error correction can help identify and remove biased or erroneous data points that may introduce bias into the model. By preprocessing the training data to reduce bias and imbalance, data scientists can improve the fairness and performance of AI models and mitigate the risk of biased predictions and discriminatory outcomes.

Moreover, model selection plays a crucial role in overcoming bias and imbalance in AI models by choosing appropriate algorithms and architectures that are robust to biased or imbalanced data. Certain machine learning algorithms, such as decision trees, support vector machines (SVM), or random forests, are inherently less susceptible to bias and imbalance compared to others, such as linear models or k-nearest neighbors (KNN), which may amplify biases present in the data. Additionally, techniques such as ensemble learning, which combine multiple models to make predictions, can help reduce bias and variance and improve the generalization ability of AI models. By carefully selecting and fine-tuning the model architecture and parameters, data scientists can develop models that are more resilient to bias and imbalance and achieve better performance on real-world datasets.

Furthermore, post-processing techniques such as bias mitigation algorithms and fairness-aware learning can be applied to AI models to correct biases and promote fairness and equity in decision-making. Bias mitigation algorithms such as demographic parity, equalized odds, or disparate impact mitigation aim to adjust model predictions to ensure fairness and equity across different demographic groups or protected attributes. Fairness-aware learning techniques incorporate fairness constraints or penalties into the model training process to explicitly optimize for fairness while minimizing prediction error. By applying post-processing techniques to AI models, data scientists can identify and correct biases in model predictions, promote fairness and equity, and build more trustworthy and accountable AI systems.

Additionally, transparency and interpretability play a crucial role in overcoming bias and imbalance in AI models by enabling stakeholders to understand how models make predictions and detect potential sources of bias or discrimination. Model-agnostic interpretability techniques such as SHAP (SHapley Additive exPlanations) or LIME (Local Interpretable Model-agnostic Explanations) can provide insights into the factors driving model predictions and help identify features or variables that contribute to biased or unfair outcomes. Additionally, transparency measures such as model documentation, algorithmic audits, and bias impact assessments can help ensure accountability and promote trust in AI systems by making the model development process more transparent and accessible to stakeholders.

Furthermore, community-driven efforts such as bias detection toolkits, benchmark datasets, and collaborative research initiatives play a crucial role in addressing bias and imbalance in AI models by providing resources, tools, and best practices for identifying, measuring, and mitigating bias in machine learning models. Open-source libraries such as AI Fairness 360, FairML, or Themis-ML offer a wide range of bias detection and mitigation algorithms, fairness metrics, and evaluation tools that enable data scientists to assess and address bias in their models. Additionally, collaborative research efforts such as the Fairness, Accountability, and Transparency in Machine Learning (FAT/ML) community and the Partnership on AI (PAI) bring together researchers, practitioners, and policymakers to address ethical and social challenges in AI and promote responsible and inclusive AI development.

In summary, overcoming bias and imbalance in AI models is crucial for building fair, reliable, and effective AI systems that can be deployed responsibly in various real-world applications. By employing a multifaceted approach that involves data preprocessing, model selection, post-processing techniques, transparency, and community-driven efforts, data scientists can mitigate bias, address class imbalance, and promote fairness, transparency, and accountability in AI systems. Overcoming bias and imbalance requires a concerted effort from stakeholders across academia, industry, and government to develop and deploy AI systems that reflect the values, priorities, and needs of diverse communities and ensure equitable and inclusive outcomes for all.

Uncertainty and ambiguity are inherent challenges in AI systems, particularly in the context of AI suggestions where the system provides recommendations or guidance to users based on incomplete or uncertain information. Uncertainty arises from various sources, including noisy data, limited domain knowledge, and inherent randomness in the environment, making it challenging for AI systems to make accurate and reliable predictions or suggestions. Ambiguity refers to the presence of multiple plausible interpretations or solutions to a given problem, leading to uncertainty about the correct course of action or decision. Dealing with uncertainty and ambiguity in AI suggestions requires robust techniques and strategies for handling uncertainty, incorporating user feedback, and enhancing the interpretability and transparency of AI systems.

One approach to dealing with uncertainty and ambiguity in AI suggestions is through probabilistic modeling and uncertainty quantification, which enables AI systems to express predictions or recommendations in terms of probability distributions rather than deterministic outcomes. Probabilistic modeling techniques such as Bayesian inference, Gaussian processes, or Monte Carlo sampling allow AI systems to capture and propagate uncertainty through the prediction process, providing users with more informative and context-aware suggestions. By quantifying uncertainty in AI suggestions, data scientists can convey the level of confidence or reliability associated with each recommendation, helping users make informed decisions and take appropriate actions based on the available evidence.

Moreover, ensemble methods such as model averaging, bagging, or boosting can help improve the robustness and reliability of AI suggestions by aggregating predictions from multiple models trained on different subsets of data or using different algorithms. Ensemble methods leverage the diversity of individual models to reduce prediction variance and enhance predictive performance, making them more resilient to uncertainty and ambiguity in the data. By combining the predictions of multiple models, ensemble methods can provide more robust and accurate suggestions, particularly in situations where individual models may exhibit different strengths and weaknesses or where the data is noisy or uncertain.

Additionally, active learning and human-in-the-loop approaches enable AI systems to interact with users and solicit feedback to improve the quality and relevance of suggestions over time. Active learning techniques such as uncertainty sampling, query synthesis, or stream-based sampling identify the most informative or uncertain data points for user feedback, allowing AI systems to focus on areas of uncertainty or ambiguity and acquire new knowledge to improve their predictive performance. By engaging users in the suggestion process and incorporating their feedback, AI systems can adapt to changing circumstances, refine their recommendations, and enhance user satisfaction and trust in the system.

Furthermore, interpretability and transparency play a crucial role in addressing uncertainty and ambiguity in AI suggestions by enabling users to understand how the system arrives at its recommendations and assess the rationale behind its decisions. Interpretability techniques such as feature importance analysis, attention mechanisms, or model-agnostic explanation methods provide insights into the factors influencing AI suggestions and help users evaluate the reliability and validity of the recommendations. By making AI systems more interpretable and transparent, data scientists can foster trust and confidence in the system, even in the presence of uncertainty and ambiguity.

Moreover, robustness testing and sensitivity analysis techniques can help assess the resilience of AI suggestions to uncertainties and variations in the input data or model parameters. Robustness testing involves subjecting AI systems to diverse and challenging scenarios to evaluate their performance under different conditions and identify potential failure modes or vulnerabilities. Sensitivity analysis techniques such as perturbation analysis, input feature importance analysis, or adversarial testing examine how changes in input data or model parameters affect the output of AI suggestions, allowing data scientists to identify sensitive features or potential sources of uncertainty and take appropriate measures to mitigate their impact.

Furthermore, uncertainty-aware decision-making frameworks such as decision theory, risk analysis, or utility theory can help users make informed decisions in the presence of uncertainty and ambiguity by explicitly considering the potential risks, costs, and benefits associated with different courses of action. Decision-theoretic approaches formalize the decision-making process by quantifying the trade-offs between different objectives and incorporating uncertainty into the decision-making process, enabling users to make rational and informed decisions based on the available evidence. By integrating uncertainty-aware decision-making frameworks into AI suggestions, data scientists can empower users to navigate uncertainty and ambiguity more effectively and make better decisions in complex and uncertain environments.

In summary, dealing with uncertainty and ambiguity in AI suggestions is a complex and multifaceted challenge that requires robust techniques and strategies for handling uncertainty, incorporating user feedback, enhancing interpretability and transparency, and enabling uncertainty-aware decision-making. By leveraging probabilistic modeling, ensemble methods, active learning, interpretability, robustness testing, sensitivity analysis, and decision-theoretic approaches, data scientists can develop AI systems that provide more reliable, informative, and context-aware suggestions, even in the presence of uncertainty and ambiguity. Overcoming uncertainty and ambiguity in AI suggestions is essential for building trustworthy, resilient, and effective AI systems that can assist users in making informed decisions and navigating uncertain and ambiguous environments.

Chapter 8: Integrating AI Pair Programming into Agile Workflows

Agile principles and AI pair programming represent complementary approaches to software development that emphasize collaboration, adaptability, and continuous improvement. Agile methodologies such as Scrum, Kanban, and Extreme Programming (XP) promote iterative development, incremental delivery, and frequent feedback loops to deliver high-quality software products that meet the evolving needs of stakeholders. AI pair programming leverages artificial intelligence (AI) techniques to enhance collaboration between developers and AI systems, enabling more efficient, productive, and insightful programming sessions. By integrating agile principles with AI pair programming practices, software development teams can streamline their development processes, improve code quality, and accelerate time-to-market while fostering a culture of collaboration, learning, and innovation.

One fundamental principle of agile development that aligns with AI pair programming is the emphasis on individuals and interactions over processes and tools. Agile methodologies prioritize human collaboration, communication, and teamwork, recognizing that effective software development requires close collaboration between developers, stakeholders, and end-users. AI pair programming builds on this principle by augmenting human developers with AI-powered tools and techniques that facilitate real-time collaboration, code suggestions, and knowledge sharing. By combining the creativity, intuition, and domain expertise of human developers with the analytical power, pattern recognition, and automation capabilities of AI systems, AI pair programming enables developers to work more effectively together, leverage each other's strengths, and produce higher-quality code.

Moreover, the agile principle of responding to change over following a plan resonates with the iterative and adaptive nature of AI pair programming. Agile methodologies advocate for embracing change, adapting to evolving requirements, and continuously improving the software product based on feedback and lessons learned. Similarly, AI pair programming supports agile development practices by providing developers with real-time feedback, suggestions, and insights that enable them to adapt and respond to changing requirements, address emerging challenges, and refine their code iteratively. By leveraging AI-powered code suggestions, refactoring tools, and debugging assistance, developers can iterate more rapidly, experiment with different solutions, and incorporate feedback from stakeholders more effectively, enhancing the agility and responsiveness of the development process.

Additionally, the agile principle of delivering working software frequently aligns with the incremental and iterative nature of AI pair programming. Agile methodologies advocate for delivering small, incremental changes to the software product on a regular basis, allowing stakeholders to provide feedback early and often and ensuring that the software evolves in alignment with the evolving needs of users. AI pair programming supports this principle by enabling developers to generate, test, and integrate code changes more rapidly, reducing the time and effort required to implement new features or fix defects. By leveraging AI-powered code generation, refactoring, and testing tools, developers can accelerate the development cycle, deliver working software more frequently, and obtain timely feedback from stakeholders, facilitating continuous improvement and adaptation.

Furthermore, the agile principle of embracing technical excellence and good design aligns with the goal of AI pair programming to improve code quality, maintainability, and readability. Agile methodologies emphasize the importance of crafting well-designed, maintainable, and scalable software solutions that meet the needs of users while minimizing technical debt and complexity. AI pair programming supports this principle by providing developers with intelligent code suggestions, refactoring recommendations, and design insights that help them write cleaner, more modular, and more maintainable code. By leveraging AI-powered code analysis and optimization tools, developers can identify and address potential code smells, anti-patterns, and design flaws early in the development process, ensuring that the software product adheres to best practices and architectural guidelines.

Moreover, the agile principle of fostering self-organizing teams resonates with the collaborative and empowering nature of AI pair programming. Agile methodologies encourage teams to self-organize, collaborate, and make collective decisions based on shared goals, values, and principles. AI pair programming supports this principle by facilitating seamless collaboration between developers and AI systems, empowering developers to make informed decisions, explore new ideas, and experiment with different approaches in a supportive and collaborative environment. By leveraging AI-powered code suggestions, pair programming assistance, and knowledge sharing tools, developers can work more autonomously, collaborate more effectively, and take ownership of their work, leading to greater creativity, engagement, and job satisfaction.

Furthermore, the agile principle of continuous improvement and reflection aligns with the learning-oriented and feedback-driven nature of AI pair programming. Agile methodologies encourage teams to reflect on their practices, processes, and outcomes regularly, identify areas for improvement, and experiment with new approaches to enhance their performance and effectiveness. AI pair programming supports this principle by providing developers with real-time feedback, suggestions, and insights that enable them to reflect on their coding practices, learn from their mistakes, and identify opportunities for improvement. By leveraging AI-powered code analysis, code review, and performance monitoring tools, developers can gain deeper insights into their coding habits, identify areas for growth, and refine their skills continuously, fostering a culture of learning, experimentation, and innovation within the development team.

In summary, agile principles and AI pair programming represent complementary approaches to software development that emphasize collaboration, adaptability, and continuous improvement. By integrating agile principles with AI pair programming practices, software development teams can streamline their development processes, improve code quality, and accelerate time-to-market while fostering a culture of collaboration, learning, and innovation. By embracing agile principles such as individuals and interactions, responding to change, delivering working software frequently, embracing technical excellence, fostering self-organizing teams, and continuous improvement, and aligning them with the capabilities and benefits of AI pair programming, organizations can create a more agile, adaptive, and effective software development environment that enables them to respond to changing market dynamics, meet customer needs, and drive business success.

Continuous Integration (CI) and Continuous Deployment (CD) practices are essential components of modern software development methodologies, enabling teams to deliver high-quality software products efficiently and reliably. CI/CD pipelines automate the process of building, testing, and deploying software changes, allowing teams to detect and address issues early in the development cycle, iterate rapidly, and deliver value to users quickly. AI assistance in CI/CD pipelines enhances automation, improves code quality, and streamlines the deployment process by leveraging AI-powered tools and techniques to augment human developers' capabilities and automate repetitive tasks.

One of the key benefits of AI assistance in CI/CD pipelines is the automation of code review and quality assurance processes. AI-powered code analysis tools can automatically scan code changes for potential issues, such as syntax errors, code smells, security vulnerabilities, or performance bottlenecks, and provide real-time feedback to developers. For example, tools like CodeClimate or SonarQube can analyze code quality metrics and provide actionable insights to help developers identify and address code quality issues before they are merged into the main codebase. By automating code review processes, AI assistance helps teams maintain code quality standards, reduce technical debt, and prevent regressions, ultimately improving the reliability and stability of software deployments.

Moreover, AI assistance in CI/CD pipelines enables intelligent test automation, allowing teams to automate the execution of various types of tests, including unit tests, integration tests, regression tests, and performance tests. AI-powered test generation tools, such as Diffblue or Parasoft, can automatically generate test cases based on code changes, identify edge cases, and prioritize tests based on their impact on the codebase. Additionally, AI-driven test execution tools, such as Applitools or Testim, can use machine learning algorithms to optimize test execution, identify flaky tests, and provide insights into test coverage and effectiveness. By automating testing processes and optimizing test coverage, AI assistance helps teams detect and address bugs early, improve software quality, and accelerate the release cycle.

Furthermore, AI assistance in CI/CD pipelines facilitates intelligent deployment automation, enabling teams to automate the process of deploying software changes to production environments seamlessly. AI-powered deployment orchestration tools, such as Harness or GitLab Auto DevOps, can analyze deployment configurations, monitor infrastructure changes, and optimize deployment strategies based on historical data and performance metrics. Additionally, AI-driven deployment validation tools, such as Rollbar or Sentry, can automatically detect deployment errors, monitor application performance, and provide real-time alerts and insights to help teams diagnose and resolve issues quickly. By automating deployment processes and providing intelligent insights, AI assistance helps teams reduce deployment errors, minimize downtime, and improve the reliability and resilience of production systems.

Moreover, AI assistance in CI/CD pipelines enables predictive analytics and anomaly detection, allowing teams to anticipate and mitigate potential issues before they impact software deployments. AI-powered monitoring and observability tools, such as Prometheus or Grafana, can analyze telemetry data, detect anomalies, and predict future trends based on historical patterns and performance metrics. Additionally, AI-driven incident management tools, such as PagerDuty or VictorOps, can prioritize incidents, route alerts to the appropriate responders, and provide recommendations for resolution based on past incidents and best practices. By leveraging predictive analytics and anomaly detection, AI assistance helps teams proactively identify and address issues, improve system reliability, and enhance the overall resilience of production environments.

Furthermore, AI assistance in CI/CD pipelines supports intelligent release management, enabling teams to optimize the release process and deliver software changes more efficiently. AI-powered release planning tools, such as Jira or Targetprocess, can analyze historical release data, predict release outcomes, and optimize release schedules based on factors such as risk, complexity, and resource availability. Additionally, AI-driven feature flagging tools, such as LaunchDarkly or Split, can enable teams to safely roll out new features, experiment with different configurations, and monitor feature usage in real-time. By automating release management processes and providing intelligent insights, AI assistance helps teams accelerate time-to-market, minimize release risk, and deliver value to users more effectively.

In summary, AI assistance in CI/CD pipelines enhances automation, improves code quality, and streamlines the deployment process by leveraging AI-powered tools and techniques to augment human developers' capabilities and automate repetitive tasks. By automating code review and quality assurance processes, enabling intelligent test automation, facilitating deployment automation, supporting predictive analytics and anomaly detection, and enabling intelligent release management, AI assistance helps teams deliver high-quality software products efficiently and reliably. By integrating AI assistance into CI/CD pipelines, organizations can improve the agility, reliability, and resilience of their software development processes, enabling them to respond to changing market dynamics, meet customer needs, and drive business success.

Chapter 9: Scaling AI Pair Programming for Large Teams

Effective team coordination and communication are crucial for the success of any project, especially in the context of software development where collaboration among team members is paramount. In today's fast-paced and distributed work environments, teams often face challenges in coordinating tasks, sharing information, and maintaining alignment across different locations and time zones. However, by adopting effective strategies for team coordination and communication, teams can overcome these challenges, foster collaboration, and achieve their goals more efficiently.

One fundamental strategy for team coordination and communication is to establish clear goals, roles, and responsibilities from the outset of the project. By defining project objectives, clarifying individual roles, and assigning responsibilities, teams can ensure that everyone understands their contributions to the project and how their work aligns with the overall goals. This can be achieved through collaborative discussions, stakeholder meetings, and documentation tools such as Confluence or Google Docs. Additionally, version control systems like Git enable teams to manage project documentation collaboratively and track changes over time, ensuring that everyone has access to the latest information.

Moreover, maintaining open and transparent communication channels is essential for effective team coordination. Teams can use a variety of communication tools and platforms to facilitate real-time communication and collaboration, such as Slack, Microsoft Teams, or Discord. These tools allow team members to share updates, ask questions, and collaborate on tasks in a centralized and accessible manner. Additionally, video conferencing tools like Zoom or Google Meet enable teams to hold virtual meetings, brainstorm ideas, and discuss project progress face-to-face, even when working remotely.

Furthermore, establishing regular communication cadences, such as daily stand-up meetings or weekly status updates, helps teams stay aligned and informed about project progress. Daily stand-up meetings, for example, provide an opportunity for team members to share their progress, discuss any blockers or challenges they are facing, and coordinate their activities for the day. Version control systems like Git also support collaboration by enabling teams to track changes to code, review each other's work, and provide feedback through pull requests and code reviews.

Additionally, fostering a culture of collaboration and knowledge sharing within the team is essential for effective team coordination. Teams can encourage collaboration by creating shared spaces for brainstorming ideas, sharing resources, and collaborating on solutions. For example, using collaborative whiteboarding tools like Miro or Lucidchart enables teams to visualize ideas, create mind maps, and collaborate on designs in real-time. Furthermore, knowledge sharing sessions, brown bag lunches, or tech talks can provide opportunities for team members to share their expertise, learn from each other, and build a collective understanding of the project domain.

Moreover, embracing agile methodologies such as Scrum or Kanban can facilitate team coordination and communication by providing frameworks for iterative development, continuous feedback, and adaptive planning. Agile ceremonies such as sprint planning, sprint reviews, and retrospectives provide opportunities for teams to synchronize their efforts, review progress, and identify areas for improvement. Project management tools like Jira or Trello support agile practices by enabling teams to plan and track their work, prioritize tasks, and visualize progress using kanban boards or sprint backlogs.

Furthermore, promoting inclusivity and diversity within the team fosters a culture of collaboration and innovation. By embracing diverse perspectives, backgrounds, and experiences, teams can generate more creative solutions, challenge assumptions, and drive positive change. Inclusive communication practices, such as active listening, empathy, and respect for different viewpoints, help create a supportive and inclusive environment where all team members feel valued and empowered to contribute.

Additionally, leveraging automation tools and workflows can streamline team coordination and communication by reducing manual overhead and enabling teams to focus on high-value tasks. For example, using CI/CD pipelines automates the process of building, testing, and deploying software changes, enabling teams to deliver value to users more efficiently. Configuration management tools like Ansible or Puppet automate infrastructure provisioning and management, reducing the risk of configuration drift and ensuring consistency across environments.

Furthermore, fostering a growth mindset within the team encourages continuous learning, experimentation, and improvement. By embracing challenges, seeking feedback, and learning from failures, teams can adapt and evolve in response to changing circumstances. Learning and development opportunities, such as workshops, training sessions, or hackathons, provide avenues for team members to acquire new skills, explore emerging technologies, and stay abreast of industry trends.

In summary, effective team coordination and communication are essential for the success of software development projects. By adopting strategies such as establishing clear goals and roles, maintaining open communication channels, establishing regular communication cadences, fostering a culture of collaboration and knowledge sharing, embracing agile methodologies, promoting inclusivity and diversity, leveraging automation tools and workflows, and fostering a growth mindset, teams can overcome challenges, foster collaboration, and achieve their goals more efficiently. By prioritizing effective team coordination and communication, organizations can build high-performing teams that deliver value to users, drive innovation, and achieve business success.

Distributed pair programming, also known as remote pair programming, has become increasingly common in today's globalized and remote-friendly work environments. With advancements in technology and communication tools, teams no longer need to be co-located to collaborate effectively on software development projects. Distributed pair programming enables developers to work together in real-time, sharing ideas, solving problems, and writing code collaboratively, regardless of their physical location. However, remote collaboration poses unique challenges compared to traditional in-person pair programming, such as communication barriers, time zone differences, and technical constraints. By adopting effective strategies and leveraging appropriate tools, teams can overcome these challenges and harness the benefits of distributed pair programming for increased productivity, improved code quality, and enhanced collaboration.

One of the key challenges in distributed pair programming is communication, as team members may be working in different time zones or cultural contexts. To overcome communication barriers, teams should establish clear communication channels and norms, such as using asynchronous communication tools like email or Slack for non-urgent messages and scheduling regular synchronous meetings for real-time discussions. Additionally, video conferencing tools like Zoom or Microsoft Teams enable face-to-face communication, fostering a sense of presence and connection among team members, even when working remotely.

Moreover, establishing a shared understanding of goals, roles, and expectations is essential for effective distributed pair programming. Teams should define project objectives, clarify individual responsibilities, and establish guidelines for collaboration to ensure alignment and accountability. Project management tools like Jira or Asana facilitate task assignment, progress tracking, and transparency, enabling teams to coordinate their activities and monitor project progress regardless of their physical location. Version control systems like Git also support collaboration by enabling teams to manage code changes, review each other's work, and track project history.

Furthermore, ensuring access to reliable and high-speed internet connectivity is crucial for effective distributed pair programming. Poor internet connectivity can disrupt communication, slow down collaboration, and hinder productivity. To mitigate this risk, teams should invest in reliable internet connections, backup options, and contingency plans, such as using mobile hotspots or offline work modes in case of internet outages. Additionally, choosing communication tools and platforms that are lightweight and optimized for low bandwidth environments can help minimize bandwidth consumption and improve performance.

Additionally, fostering a culture of trust, transparency, and inclusivity is essential for successful distributed pair programming. Teams should encourage open communication, active participation, and mutual respect among team members, regardless of their physical location. Inclusive communication practices, such as active listening, empathy, and respect for diverse viewpoints, help create a supportive and inclusive environment where all team members feel valued and empowered to contribute. Moreover, regular team-building activities, virtual coffee breaks, or informal hangouts can help foster social connections and strengthen team bonds, despite the physical distance.

Moreover, leveraging remote collaboration tools and technologies can enhance the effectiveness of distributed pair programming. Integrated development environments (IDEs) like Visual Studio Code or JetBrains IntelliJ IDEA support real-time collaborative editing and debugging, enabling developers to work together on the same codebase simultaneously. Screen sharing and remote control tools like TeamViewer or AnyDesk allow developers to share their screens, demonstrate concepts, and troubleshoot issues collaboratively. Additionally, cloud-based development platforms like GitHub or GitLab provide centralized repositories, version control, and collaboration features, enabling teams to collaborate on code changes seamlessly.

Furthermore, establishing clear workflows and conventions for remote pair programming helps streamline collaboration and ensure consistency across team members. Teams should agree on coding standards, naming conventions, and code review processes to maintain code quality and readability. Pair programming sessions should have defined roles, such as driver and navigator, to ensure a balanced distribution of tasks and responsibilities. Additionally, establishing regular checkpoints and milestones helps track progress, identify bottlenecks, and adjust strategies as needed to meet project deadlines and goals.

In summary, distributed pair programming offers numerous benefits for teams, including increased productivity, improved code quality, and enhanced collaboration. By adopting effective strategies such as establishing clear communication channels and norms, defining project objectives and roles, ensuring reliable internet connectivity, fostering a culture of trust and inclusivity, leveraging remote collaboration tools and technologies, and establishing clear workflows and conventions, teams can overcome the challenges of remote collaboration and harness the benefits of distributed pair programming for successful software development projects. By embracing distributed pair programming, organizations can tap into a global talent pool, foster innovation, and achieve their business objectives in today's digital economy.

Chapter 10: Emerging Trends in AI Pair Programming Research

In recent years, AI-assisted programming has witnessed significant advancements, driven by cutting-edge research in artificial intelligence, machine learning, and natural language processing. Researchers and developers are continuously pushing the boundaries of what is possible with AI, exploring new techniques, algorithms, and models to enhance the capabilities of AI-powered programming tools. This relentless pursuit of innovation is fueled by a growing demand for more efficient, reliable, and intelligent programming assistance tools that can help developers write code faster, reduce errors, and tackle increasingly complex software development challenges.

One area of cutting-edge research in AI-assisted programming is the development of advanced natural language understanding models. These models, such as GPT (Generative Pre-trained Transformer) and BERT (Bidirectional Encoder Representations from Transformers), are trained on vast amounts of text data to understand and generate human-like text. By fine-tuning these pre-trained language models on code-related tasks and domains, researchers can create AI models that are specifically tailored to assist developers in writing code, understanding code snippets, and providing contextually relevant suggestions. For example, OpenAI's Codex, based on GPT, has demonstrated remarkable capabilities in understanding and generating code based on natural language prompts.

Moreover, researchers are exploring techniques to improve the accuracy and relevance of AI-generated code suggestions. One approach is to leverage semantic code search techniques, which analyze the meaning and intent behind code snippets to retrieve relevant examples or solutions from code repositories. By incorporating semantic understanding into AI-powered programming tools, developers can receive more contextually relevant suggestions that align with their coding objectives and requirements. Additionally, techniques such as code summarization and abstraction help condense complex code snippets into more manageable and understandable representations, facilitating code comprehension and reuse.

Furthermore, researchers are investigating methods to enhance the adaptability and personalization of AI-assisted programming tools. One approach is to develop AI models that can adapt to individual coding styles, preferences, and contexts, providing personalized recommendations and suggestions tailored to each developer's unique needs. This requires incorporating user feedback mechanisms into AI models, enabling them to learn from developer interactions and refine their recommendations over time. Additionally, researchers are exploring techniques to enable collaborative AI programming, where AI systems can collaborate with developers in real-time, assisting them in brainstorming ideas, exploring alternative solutions, and co-authoring code.

Additionally, researchers are exploring ways to address ethical and fairness considerations in AI-assisted programming. As AI models become more pervasive in software development workflows, there is a growing awareness of the potential biases and ethical implications associated with their use. Researchers are working to develop techniques for bias detection and mitigation in AI models, ensuring that they do not perpetuate or amplify existing biases in codebases or programming practices. Moreover, efforts are underway to promote transparency and accountability in AI-powered programming tools, enabling developers to understand how AI models make decisions and providing mechanisms for auditing and debugging their behavior.

Furthermore, researchers are exploring novel applications of AI in software testing, debugging, and maintenance. AI-powered testing tools leverage techniques such as automated test generation, fault localization, and test case prioritization to improve the efficiency and effectiveness of software testing processes. By harnessing the power of AI to automate repetitive tasks, identify potential bugs, and prioritize testing efforts, developers can accelerate the delivery of high-quality software products while minimizing the risk of defects and regressions. Additionally, AI-powered debugging tools analyze program execution traces, identify root causes of errors, and provide actionable insights to help developers diagnose and fix bugs more efficiently.

Moreover, researchers are investigating techniques to enhance the interpretability and explainability of AI-generated code suggestions. As AI-powered programming tools become more sophisticated, there is a growing need for developers to understand how AI models arrive at their recommendations and suggestions. Techniques such as attention mechanisms, saliency maps, and model introspection enable developers to interpret and visualize the decision-making process of AI models, gaining insights into their inner workings and building trust in their recommendations. By enhancing the interpretability of AI-powered programming tools, developers can make more informed decisions and leverage AI assistance more effectively in their workflows.

In summary, cutting-edge research in AI-assisted programming is driving innovation and reshaping the landscape of software development. By pushing the boundaries of AI, machine learning, and natural language processing, researchers are developing advanced AI models and techniques that can assist developers in writing code, understanding code snippets, and collaborating more effectively. Moreover, researchers are addressing ethical considerations, promoting transparency and fairness, and exploring novel applications of AI in software testing, debugging, and maintenance. As AI-powered programming tools continue to evolve, they have the potential to revolutionize the way software is developed, enabling developers to build better, faster, and more reliable software products in an increasingly complex and interconnected world.

The future of AI-assisted programming holds immense promise, with researchers and developers exploring new avenues and potential breakthroughs that could revolutionize software development practices. As AI technologies continue to advance rapidly, there are several key areas where significant progress and innovation are expected in the coming years, paving the way for transformative changes in how code is written, tested, and maintained.

One area of focus for future research and development in AI-assisted programming is the integration of domain-specific knowledge and context-awareness into AI models. While current AI-powered programming tools have demonstrated impressive capabilities in understanding and generating code based on natural language prompts, they often lack domain-specific expertise and struggle to provide contextually relevant suggestions in specialized domains or industries. To address this challenge, researchers are exploring techniques to incorporate domain-specific knowledge bases, ontologies, and domain-specific languages into AI models, enabling them to better understand and generate code tailored to specific application domains, such as finance, healthcare, or cybersecurity. By augmenting AI models with domain-specific knowledge, developers can receive more accurate, relevant, and actionable suggestions that align with the requirements and constraints of their respective domains.

Moreover, researchers are investigating methods to improve the interpretability and explainability of AI-generated code suggestions. While AI-powered programming tools can provide valuable assistance to developers in writing code, understanding code snippets, and debugging software, they often operate as black boxes, making it challenging for developers to understand how they arrive at their recommendations and suggestions. To address this limitation, researchers are developing techniques for model introspection, attention visualization, and explanation generation, enabling developers to interpret and understand the decision-making process of AI models. By enhancing the interpretability and explainability of AI-powered programming tools, developers can gain insights into the inner workings of AI models, build trust in their recommendations, and make more informed decisions about when and how to leverage AI assistance in their workflows.

Furthermore, researchers are exploring techniques to enable collaborative AI programming, where AI systems can collaborate with developers in real-time, assisting them in brainstorming ideas, exploring alternative solutions, and co-authoring code. While current AI-powered programming tools primarily operate in a solo mode, providing suggestions and recommendations to individual developers, the future holds the potential for more interactive and collaborative modes of interaction between humans and AI systems. By enabling seamless collaboration between developers and AI systems, teams can leverage the complementary strengths of humans and machines, fostering creativity, innovation, and productivity in software development projects.

Additionally, researchers are investigating methods to enhance the adaptability and personalization of AI-assisted programming tools. One approach is to develop AI models that can adapt to individual coding styles, preferences, and contexts, providing personalized recommendations and suggestions tailored to each developer's unique needs. This requires incorporating user feedback mechanisms into AI models, enabling them to learn from developer interactions and refine their recommendations over time. By personalizing AI assistance to the needs and preferences of individual developers, teams can maximize the effectiveness and utility of AI-powered programming tools, empowering developers to write better code faster and more efficiently.

Moreover, researchers are exploring the potential of AI-powered programming tools to automate repetitive coding tasks, such as code generation, refactoring, and bug fixing. While current AI-assisted programming tools provide valuable assistance to developers in writing code, they often require manual intervention and oversight to ensure the correctness and quality of generated code. In the future, AI models could become increasingly capable of automating repetitive coding tasks, leveraging techniques such as reinforcement learning, automated planning, and program synthesis to generate high-quality code autonomously. By automating repetitive coding tasks, developers can focus their time and energy on more creative and high-value aspects of software development, such as architecture design, algorithmic optimization, and problem-solving.

Furthermore, researchers are exploring novel applications of AI in software testing, debugging, and maintenance. AI-powered testing tools leverage techniques such as automated test generation, fault localization, and test case prioritization to improve the efficiency and effectiveness of software testing processes. By harnessing the power of AI to automate repetitive tasks, identify potential bugs, and prioritize testing efforts, developers can accelerate the delivery of high-quality software products while minimizing the risk of defects and regressions. Additionally, AI-powered debugging tools analyze program execution traces, identify root causes of errors, and provide actionable insights to help developers diagnose and fix bugs more efficiently.

In summary, the future of AI-assisted programming is filled with exciting possibilities and potential breakthroughs that could reshape the landscape of software development. By incorporating domain-specific knowledge, enhancing interpretability and explainability, enabling collaborative AI programming, personalizing AI assistance, automating repetitive coding tasks, and exploring novel applications of AI in software testing and debugging, researchers and developers are paving the way for more intelligent, efficient, and productive software development workflows. As AI technologies continue to advance, the boundaries of what is possible in AI-assisted programming will continue to expand, unlocking new opportunities for innovation and creativity in software development.

BOOK 3
EFFICIENT CODING WITH GITHUB COPILOT STRATEGIES
FOR INTERMEDIATE DEVELOPERS

ROB BOTWRIGHT

Chapter 1: Maximizing Productivity with GitHub Copilot

GitHub Copilot offers a plethora of productivity features designed to streamline the coding process, boost efficiency, and facilitate collaboration among developers. These features encompass a wide range of functionalities, from code completion and suggestions to customization options and collaboration tools. By mastering Copilot's productivity features, developers can accelerate their workflow, write better code, and collaborate more effectively with their peers.

One of Copilot's core productivity features is its intelligent code completion and suggestion system, which leverages advanced AI models to provide contextually relevant code snippets and suggestions as developers write code. This feature is invaluable for speeding up the coding process and reducing manual effort, as developers can quickly insert pre-written code snippets, function calls, or entire blocks of code with just a few keystrokes. For example, when working on a web development project, developers can use Copilot to generate HTML, CSS, and JavaScript code snippets for common tasks such as creating forms, styling elements, or handling user input.

Moreover, Copilot's code completion and suggestion system is not limited to basic syntax or language constructs but can also assist with more complex coding tasks, such as implementing algorithms, designing data structures, or integrating with external APIs. This versatility makes Copilot a powerful ally for developers tackling a wide range of programming challenges, from simple scripting tasks to complex software engineering projects. For instance, developers working on a machine learning project can use Copilot to generate code for data preprocessing, model training, and evaluation, saving time and effort in implementing standard machine learning workflows.

Additionally, Copilot offers customization options that allow developers to tailor its behavior and suggestions to their specific preferences and coding style. For example, developers can configure Copilot to prioritize certain coding patterns or libraries, adjust the level of verbosity in generated code, or enable/disable specific features based on their workflow requirements. These customization options empower developers to fine-tune Copilot to suit their individual needs and coding preferences, enhancing their productivity and overall coding experience.

Furthermore, Copilot includes built-in collaboration features that enable developers to share code snippets, collaborate on coding tasks, and review each other's code directly within their development environment. For instance, developers can use Copilot to create shared code notebooks, where multiple team members can simultaneously edit and execute code in real-time, facilitating collaborative coding sessions and pair programming exercises. Additionally, Copilot integrates seamlessly with GitHub's collaboration tools, allowing developers to create pull requests, review code changes, and provide feedback to their peers without leaving their IDE.

Moreover, Copilot's productivity features extend beyond code generation and collaboration to include tools for code navigation, documentation lookup, and error handling. For example, developers can use Copilot to navigate large codebases more efficiently by quickly jumping to definitions, references, or usages of specific variables or functions. Similarly, Copilot can assist developers in understanding unfamiliar code by providing inline documentation, examples, and usage tips for libraries, APIs, or language features. Additionally, Copilot can help developers diagnose and fix errors in their code by suggesting common solutions, debugging techniques, or alternative approaches based on contextual information and code analysis.

Furthermore, Copilot's productivity features are continuously evolving and improving through ongoing updates and enhancements driven by user feedback and advances in AI research. GitHub actively solicits input from developers and incorporates their suggestions and feature requests into future releases of Copilot, ensuring that it remains a valuable tool for developers worldwide. Additionally, GitHub invests in research and development efforts to further enhance Copilot's capabilities and address emerging trends and challenges in software development, such as the rise of new programming languages, frameworks, and paradigms.

In summary, understanding Copilot's productivity features is essential for developers looking to harness the full potential of this powerful AI-assisted programming tool. By mastering Copilot's code completion and suggestion system, customization options, collaboration features, code navigation tools, documentation lookup capabilities, and error handling tools, developers can accelerate their workflow, write better code, and collaborate more effectively with their peers. As Copilot continues to evolve and improve, it will play an increasingly important role in shaping the future of software development, empowering developers to build better software faster and more efficiently than ever before.

GitHub Copilot offers a multitude of time-saving strategies that developers can implement to streamline their coding workflow and boost productivity. These strategies leverage Copilot's AI-powered code generation capabilities, customization options, collaboration tools, and other productivity features to help developers save time and effort when writing code. By incorporating these strategies into their development process, developers can optimize their workflow, write better code faster, and focus on solving complex problems rather than repetitive tasks.

One effective time-saving strategy with Copilot is leveraging its code completion and suggestion system to quickly generate boilerplate code, repetitive code snippets, or commonly used functions. By simply typing a few keywords or phrases, developers can prompt Copilot to generate code snippets that match their current context, reducing the need to manually write or copy-paste code from other sources. For example, when working on a web development project, developers can use Copilot to generate HTML tags, CSS styles, or JavaScript functions for common UI elements, such as buttons, forms, or navigation menus, saving time and effort in writing repetitive code.

Moreover, developers can use Copilot's customization options to tailor its suggestions and recommendations to their specific coding style, preferences, and project requirements. For instance, developers can configure Copilot to prioritize certain coding patterns, libraries, or frameworks, ensuring that its suggestions align with their preferred development stack. Additionally, developers can adjust the verbosity level of Copilot's generated code, choosing between concise, readable, or verbose code snippets based on their personal preference or project constraints. By customizing Copilot to suit their individual needs, developers can streamline their coding workflow and write code more efficiently.

Another time-saving strategy with Copilot is using its collaboration features to facilitate real-time code reviews, pair programming sessions, or collaborative coding exercises with team members. Copilot integrates seamlessly with GitHub's collaboration tools, allowing developers to create shared code notebooks, review code changes, and provide feedback to their peers directly within their development environment. For example, developers can use Copilot to invite team members to a collaborative coding session, where multiple developers can simultaneously edit and execute code, discuss implementation details, and brainstorm solutions to coding challenges in real-time. By leveraging Copilot's collaboration features, teams can enhance their productivity, foster collaboration, and accelerate the development process.

Furthermore, developers can use Copilot to automate repetitive coding tasks, such as code refactoring, code generation, or code formatting, using custom code templates and shortcuts. Copilot allows developers to create custom code templates for common coding patterns, design patterns, or architectural styles, enabling them to quickly scaffold new code or refactor existing code with just a few keystrokes. Additionally, developers can define custom shortcuts or aliases for frequently used code snippets, functions, or commands, making it easier to insert boilerplate code or execute common tasks with minimal effort. By automating repetitive coding tasks with Copilot, developers can save time and focus on more challenging aspects of software development.

Moreover, developers can use Copilot's advanced code analysis and error detection capabilities to identify and fix common coding mistakes, syntax errors, or logical inconsistencies in their code. Copilot can analyze code in real-time, providing instant feedback and suggestions to help developers improve code quality, readability, and maintainability. For example, Copilot can flag potential bugs, unused variables, or inefficient code patterns, enabling developers to address these issues proactively before they escalate into larger problems. By leveraging Copilot's code analysis and error detection features, developers can write cleaner, more reliable code and minimize the time spent debugging and troubleshooting.

Additionally, developers can use Copilot to explore alternative solutions, design patterns, or implementation strategies for complex coding problems, leveraging its vast repository of code examples, libraries, and APIs. Copilot can provide insights and recommendations based on contextual information and best practices, helping developers make informed decisions about the most appropriate approach to solving a particular problem. For example, Copilot can suggest alternative algorithms, data structures, or optimization techniques for performance-critical code sections, enabling developers to choose the most efficient solution for their specific use case. By leveraging Copilot's expertise and knowledge, developers can expedite the problem-solving process and make better decisions when designing and implementing software solutions.

Furthermore, developers can use Copilot's language support and integration capabilities to work seamlessly across multiple programming languages, frameworks, and development environments. Copilot supports a wide range of programming languages, including popular languages such as Python, JavaScript, Java, C++, and Ruby, as well as niche languages and domain-specific languages. Additionally, Copilot integrates with popular IDEs, text editors, and development platforms, allowing developers to access its features directly within their preferred coding environment. By leveraging Copilot's language support and integration capabilities, developers can write code in their preferred language and environment without having to switch between different tools or contexts, saving time and reducing context-switching overhead.

In summary, implementing time-saving strategies with Copilot can significantly improve developers' productivity and efficiency by streamlining their coding workflow, automating repetitive tasks, facilitating collaboration, and providing intelligent code suggestions and recommendations. By leveraging Copilot's AI-powered code generation capabilities, customization options, collaboration features, code analysis tools, and language support, developers can optimize their development process and focus on solving complex problems rather than mundane tasks. As Copilot continues to evolve and improve, it will remain an invaluable tool for developers seeking to write better code faster and more efficiently.

Chapter 2: Understanding Intermediate Coding Challenges

As developers progress from beginners to intermediate level, they encounter a new set of challenges and hurdles in their coding journey. These challenges often arise from the complexity of the projects they undertake, the need for deeper understanding of programming concepts, and the transition from following tutorials to independently solving problems. Identifying and overcoming these common intermediate level coding hurdles is crucial for developers to continue advancing their skills and becoming proficient in their craft.

One common intermediate level coding hurdle is mastering data structures and algorithms. While beginners may have a basic understanding of data types such as arrays and strings, intermediate developers need to delve deeper into more complex data structures like linked lists, trees, graphs, and hash tables. Additionally, they must learn various algorithms for sorting, searching, and traversing these data structures efficiently. To address this hurdle, developers can use online resources, textbooks, and coding platforms to study and practice implementing different data structures and algorithms. For example, they can use the command git clone to clone repositories containing coding challenges and solutions, then run the code locally to understand how algorithms work in practice.

Another common challenge for intermediate developers is understanding and implementing object-oriented programming (OOP) concepts effectively. OOP principles such as encapsulation, inheritance, and polymorphism are fundamental to building scalable and maintainable software systems. However, transitioning from procedural programming to OOP can be daunting for developers at this stage. To overcome this hurdle, developers can create small projects or refactor existing codebases to apply OOP principles in practice. They can use CLI commands like git diff to compare changes made during refactoring and ensure that the code adheres to OOP best practices.

Furthermore, intermediate developers often struggle with debugging and troubleshooting more complex codebases. As projects grow in size and complexity, identifying and fixing bugs becomes increasingly challenging. Developers may encounter issues related to logic errors, runtime exceptions, or unexpected behavior caused by interactions between different components of the system. To address this hurdle, developers can use debugging tools provided by their IDEs or text editors to step through code execution, inspect variable values, and identify the root cause of errors. For example, they can use the command debug in IDEs like Visual Studio Code or PyCharm to start a debugging session and set breakpoints at specific lines of code.

Additionally, intermediate developers may face challenges related to code organization and modularity. As projects become larger and more complex, maintaining a clean and modular codebase becomes essential for readability, scalability, and collaboration. However, without proper planning and architectural design, codebases can quickly become messy and difficult to maintain. To overcome this hurdle, developers can adopt software design patterns such as MVC (Model-View-Controller), MVVM (Model-View-ViewModel), or Dependency Injection to structure their code in a more modular and maintainable way. They can use CLI commands like npm install or pip install to add third-party libraries that provide implementations of these design patterns, then refactor their code to leverage these libraries effectively.

Moreover, intermediate developers often struggle with version control and collaboration workflows, especially when working on projects with multiple team members. Understanding concepts such as branching, merging, and resolving conflicts is essential for effective collaboration using version control systems like Git. Additionally, developers need to learn how to use collaboration platforms like GitHub or GitLab to manage project repositories, create pull requests, and review code changes. To address this hurdle, developers can use online tutorials, documentation, and interactive exercises to learn Git and GitHub basics. They can use CLI commands like git branch, git merge, and git pull to manage branches and synchronize changes with remote repositories.

Furthermore, intermediate developers may encounter challenges related to performance optimization and resource management in their code. As projects scale in size and complexity, issues such as memory leaks, CPU bottlenecks, and inefficient algorithms can degrade system performance and user experience. To address this hurdle, developers can use profiling tools to identify performance bottlenecks and optimize critical sections of their code. For example, they can use the command npm audit to identify vulnerabilities in Node.js packages and pipenv check to check for security vulnerabilities in Python dependencies.

Additionally, intermediate developers may struggle with staying up-to-date with the latest technologies and industry trends. The field of software development is constantly evolving, with new languages, frameworks, and tools emerging regularly. To overcome this hurdle, developers can invest time in continuous learning and professional development. They can follow industry blogs, attend conferences and meetups, and participate in online communities to stay informed about new developments in their field. They can use CLI commands like npm outdated or pip list --outdated to check for outdated dependencies in their projects and update them to the latest versions.

In summary, identifying and overcoming common intermediate level coding hurdles is essential for developers to progress in their careers and become proficient software engineers. By mastering concepts such as data structures and algorithms, object-oriented programming, debugging and troubleshooting, code organization and modularity, version control and collaboration workflows, performance optimization, and continuous learning, developers can overcome these challenges and continue to grow as professionals. By leveraging online resources, interactive tutorials, coding platforms, and version control systems effectively, developers can build the skills and knowledge needed to succeed in today's competitive software development industry.

As developers progress beyond the beginner stage and enter the intermediate phase of their coding journey, they encounter a range of challenges that require strategic approaches to overcome. These challenges can arise from various sources, including the complexity of projects, deeper technical concepts, and the need for more sophisticated problem-solving skills. In navigating these hurdles, developers can employ a set of effective strategies tailored to their specific needs and circumstances.

One of the primary challenges that intermediate developers face is mastering more advanced programming concepts, such as data structures and algorithms. These foundational concepts form the backbone of software development and are essential for solving complex problems efficiently. To overcome this challenge, developers can adopt a structured learning approach, focusing on one concept at a time and practicing extensively until they achieve mastery. Online platforms like LeetCode, HackerRank, and CodeSignal offer a plethora of coding challenges and exercises tailored to different skill levels, allowing developers to reinforce their understanding and build confidence in tackling more challenging problems. Additionally, developers can leverage resources such as textbooks, online courses, and interactive tutorials to deepen their understanding of data structures and algorithms. By dedicating time and effort to deliberate practice and continuous learning, developers can gradually overcome this hurdle and become proficient in these critical areas.

Another common challenge for intermediate developers is transitioning from writing simple scripts to building larger, more complex applications. As projects grow in size and scope, developers must grapple with issues related to code organization, scalability, and maintainability. To address this challenge, developers can adopt software engineering best practices and design principles that facilitate modular, well-structured codebases. For example, they can apply architectural patterns like MVC (Model-View-Controller) or MVVM (Model-View-ViewModel) to decouple components and improve code maintainability. Furthermore, developers can embrace tools and frameworks that provide built-in support for features like dependency injection, routing, and state management, simplifying the process of building and maintaining large-scale applications. By following established design patterns and leveraging modern development tools, developers can navigate the complexities of building robust, scalable software solutions more effectively.

Additionally, intermediate developers often encounter challenges related to debugging and troubleshooting complex codebases. As projects become more intricate, identifying and fixing bugs becomes increasingly challenging, requiring developers to employ a systematic approach to problem-solving. One effective strategy for overcoming this challenge is adopting a methodical debugging process that involves isolating the problem, gathering relevant information, formulating hypotheses, and testing potential solutions systematically. Tools like debuggers, logging frameworks, and profiling utilities can aid developers in diagnosing and resolving issues more efficiently. Furthermore, developers can leverage version control systems like Git to track changes and revert to previous states when troubleshooting complex issues. By approaching debugging as a structured problem-solving exercise and utilizing appropriate tools and techniques, developers can overcome this hurdle and maintain the stability and reliability of their codebases.

Moreover, intermediate developers often face challenges in collaborating effectively with team members on shared codebases. As projects grow in scope and complexity, coordinating development efforts becomes increasingly important, requiring effective communication, coordination, and version control practices. To address this challenge, developers can adopt agile methodologies and collaborative development workflows that emphasize transparency, communication, and iterative development. Tools like GitLab, Bitbucket, and GitHub provide features such as pull requests, code reviews, and issue tracking that facilitate collaboration and code sharing among team members. Additionally, developers can establish coding standards, documentation practices, and peer review processes to ensure consistency and quality across their codebase. By embracing collaborative development practices and leveraging appropriate tools and workflows, developers can overcome the challenges of working in a team environment and deliver high-quality software more effectively.

Furthermore, intermediate developers may encounter challenges related to time management and prioritization as they juggle multiple tasks and deadlines. To overcome this challenge, developers can adopt time management techniques and productivity strategies that help them stay organized and focused. Techniques such as the Pomodoro Technique, time blocking, and task prioritization can help developers allocate their time effectively and maintain a productive workflow. Additionally, developers can leverage project management tools like Trello, Asana, or Jira to track tasks, set deadlines, and collaborate with team members more efficiently. By developing strong time management skills and implementing effective productivity strategies, developers can overcome the challenge of managing competing priorities and meet project deadlines more consistently.

In summary, overcoming intermediate coding challenges requires a combination of strategic thinking, continuous learning, and effective problem-solving skills. By focusing on mastering foundational concepts, adopting best practices in software engineering, honing debugging and troubleshooting abilities, embracing collaborative development practices, and developing strong time management skills, developers can navigate the complexities of software development more effectively and achieve greater success in their careers. Through dedication, perseverance, and a commitment to growth and improvement, intermediate developers can overcome any obstacle they encounter on their coding journey and continue to evolve and excel in their craft.

Chapter 3: Leveraging Copilot for Efficient Debugging

Debugging is an essential skill for developers, allowing them to identify and fix errors in their code efficiently. As software projects become more complex, debugging can become increasingly challenging, requiring developers to leverage various tools and techniques to diagnose and resolve issues effectively. In recent years, the advent of AI-powered coding assistants like GitHub Copilot has introduced new possibilities for streamlining the debugging process. By harnessing the power of machine learning and natural language processing, Copilot can provide insightful suggestions and recommendations to assist developers in debugging their code. Next, we explore a range of debugging techniques that leverage Copilot suggestions to enhance the debugging process and improve productivity.

One fundamental debugging technique that developers often use is logging. Logging involves inserting statements into the codebase to output relevant information at runtime, allowing developers to track the flow of execution and identify potential issues. When faced with a bug, developers can leverage Copilot to generate logging statements tailored to the context of the problem. For example, if a variable is unexpectedly null at a certain point in the code, developers can use Copilot to suggest logging statements that output the value of the variable along with contextual information. By strategically placing logging statements in the codebase and analyzing the resulting logs, developers can gain insights into the behavior of the program and pinpoint the root cause of the bug more effectively.

Another common debugging technique is breakpoint debugging, which involves pausing the execution of the program at specific points to inspect the state of the program and analyze its behavior. Breakpoint debugging is particularly useful for isolating and diagnosing complex bugs that are difficult to reproduce consistently. With Copilot, developers can leverage its suggestions to set breakpoints dynamically based on the context of the problem. For instance, if a bug occurs only under certain conditions or when specific variables reach certain values, developers can use Copilot to generate breakpoint conditions that trigger the debugger when these conditions are met. By strategically setting breakpoints and analyzing the program's state at each breakpoint, developers can gain valuable insights into the program's execution flow and identify the cause of the bug more efficiently.

Additionally, developers often use unit tests as a proactive debugging technique to catch bugs early in the development process. Unit tests involve writing automated tests to verify the correctness of individual components or functions within the codebase. By running these tests regularly as part of the development workflow, developers can detect regressions and unexpected behavior quickly. With Copilot, developers can generate unit test templates and assertions based on the code under test, allowing them to create comprehensive test suites more efficiently. For example, if a function is expected to return a specific value under certain conditions, developers can use Copilot to generate assertions that verify the function's behavior. By automating the generation of unit tests with Copilot, developers can ensure better test coverage and more robust code quality.

Furthermore, developers can leverage Copilot suggestions to perform dynamic code analysis and refactorings to improve the maintainability and readability of their codebase. Copilot can provide recommendations for code refactorings, such as extracting duplicate code into reusable functions, renaming variables and functions for clarity, and simplifying complex expressions or control flow structures. By incorporating Copilot suggestions into their refactoring workflow, developers can make their codebase more manageable and reduce the likelihood of introducing new bugs during the refactoring process.

Moreover, Copilot can assist developers in troubleshooting runtime errors by providing contextual suggestions for handling exceptions and error conditions gracefully. When faced with an unhandled exception or unexpected error, developers can use Copilot to generate error-handling code snippets that capture relevant information about the error, log it appropriately, and provide feedback to the user if necessary. By leveraging Copilot's suggestions for error handling, developers can improve the resilience and robustness of their applications and provide a better user experience.

Additionally, Copilot can help developers identify and fix common performance bottlenecks in their codebase by suggesting optimizations and best practices. For example, if a piece of code is executing slowly due to inefficient algorithms or data structures, Copilot can provide recommendations for optimizing the code for better performance. By incorporating Copilot's suggestions for performance optimization into their workflow, developers can ensure that their applications are responsive and efficient, even under heavy loads.

In summary, debugging techniques with Copilot suggestions offer developers powerful tools for diagnosing and fixing bugs, improving code quality, and enhancing productivity. By leveraging Copilot's AI-powered capabilities to generate logging statements, set breakpoints, create unit tests, perform code analysis and refactorings, handle exceptions gracefully, and optimize performance, developers can streamline the debugging process and accelerate the development cycle. However, it's essential to remember that while Copilot can provide valuable assistance, it's not a substitute for critical thinking and domain expertise. Developers should use Copilot suggestions as a supplement to their debugging toolkit and validate the suggestions in the context of their specific problem and project requirements. By combining human ingenuity with AI-powered automation, developers can overcome debugging challenges more effectively and deliver high-quality software products that meet user expectations.

Automated testing and debugging are integral components of the software development process, enabling developers to verify the correctness and reliability of their code efficiently. By automating the testing and debugging tasks, developers can identify and fix errors early in the development cycle, streamline the software delivery process, and improve overall code quality. With the integration of Copilot, an AI-powered coding assistant developed by GitHub and OpenAI, developers can enhance their automated testing and debugging workflows by leveraging Copilot's intelligent suggestions and recommendations.

One of the primary benefits of integrating Copilot into automated testing workflows is its ability to generate test cases and assertions based on the code under test. By analyzing the structure and behavior of the code, Copilot can provide insights into potential edge cases, boundary conditions, and error scenarios that developers may overlook. For example, when writing unit tests for a function that performs arithmetic operations, Copilot can suggest test cases to cover various input values, including positive, negative, zero, and boundary values, as well as edge cases such as division by zero or overflow conditions. By incorporating Copilot's test case suggestions into their testing suite, developers can improve test coverage and ensure that their code is thoroughly tested under different scenarios.

Moreover, Copilot can assist developers in writing test assertions that verify the expected behavior of the code. Assertions are statements that validate the outcome of a test case by comparing the actual result with the expected result. With Copilot's assistance, developers can generate assertions that check for specific conditions, such as equality, inequality, truthiness, or the presence of certain elements in data structures. For instance, when testing a sorting algorithm, Copilot can suggest assertions to verify that the output array is sorted in ascending or descending order, contains the same elements as the input array, and does not contain any additional or missing elements. By leveraging Copilot's suggestions for test assertions, developers can ensure that their tests are comprehensive and accurately verify the behavior of their code.

Additionally, Copilot can aid developers in automating the generation of mock objects and stubs for unit testing purposes. Mock objects are simulated objects that mimic the behavior of real objects in a controlled environment, allowing developers to isolate the code under test and verify its interactions with dependencies. By analyzing the codebase and understanding its dependencies, Copilot can generate mock objects and stubs tailored to the specific context of the test scenario. For example, when testing a function that interacts with a database, Copilot can suggest mock objects that simulate database queries and responses, allowing developers to test the function's behavior without relying on a real database connection. By automating the generation of mock objects with Copilot, developers can accelerate the creation of unit tests and ensure that their code is tested in isolation from external dependencies.

Furthermore, Copilot can assist developers in debugging test failures by providing insights into the root cause of the failure and suggesting potential fixes. When a test fails, developers can analyze the error message and stack trace to identify the source of the problem. With Copilot's assistance, developers can generate debugging statements, logging messages, and error-handling code to diagnose and troubleshoot the issue effectively. For example, if a test fails due to an unexpected exception, Copilot can suggest try-catch blocks to handle the exception gracefully, log relevant information about the error, and provide feedback to the user. By leveraging Copilot's suggestions for debugging, developers can expedite the resolution of test failures and ensure the reliability of their test suite.

Moreover, Copilot can aid developers in automating the generation of test documentation and reports, facilitating communication and collaboration among team members. Test documentation typically includes information about the test scenarios, expected outcomes, test results, and any relevant observations or comments. With Copilot's assistance, developers can generate test documentation templates and fill in the details based on the test scenarios and assertions. For instance, Copilot can suggest boilerplate text for test case descriptions, input values, expected outcomes, and actual results, allowing developers to create comprehensive and well-structured test reports efficiently. By automating the generation of test documentation with Copilot, developers can streamline the documentation process and ensure that test results are documented accurately and consistently.

In summary, integrating Copilot into automated testing and debugging workflows offers developers a powerful tool for improving code quality, productivity, and reliability. By leveraging Copilot's intelligent suggestions for test cases, assertions, mock objects, debugging, and documentation, developers can streamline the testing process, accelerate the identification and resolution of bugs, and ensure that their code meets the desired quality standards. However, it's essential to remember that while Copilot can provide valuable assistance, it's not a substitute for critical thinking and domain expertise. Developers should use Copilot's suggestions as a supplement to their testing and debugging toolkit and validate the suggestions in the context of their specific project requirements. By combining human ingenuity with AI-powered automation, developers can leverage Copilot's capabilities to enhance their testing and debugging workflows and deliver high-quality software products that meet user expectations.

Chapter 4: Advanced Code Refactoring Techniques

Code refactoring is a fundamental practice in software development aimed at improving the structure, readability, and maintainability of code without altering its external behavior. Effective code refactoring involves making incremental changes to the codebase to eliminate redundancy, improve clarity, and enhance extensibility, thereby facilitating easier maintenance and future development. Next, we explore the principles of effective code refactoring and discuss strategies for identifying opportunities for refactoring, prioritizing refactoring efforts, and applying refactoring techniques to refactor code efficiently and safely.

One of the key principles of effective code refactoring is to refactor early and refactor often. By refactoring code regularly throughout the development process, developers can address technical debt and prevent it from accumulating over time. Refactoring early allows developers to maintain a clean and maintainable codebase from the outset, reducing the likelihood of encountering issues later in the development lifecycle. To refactor code early, developers should integrate refactoring into their daily workflow and allocate time for refactoring tasks alongside feature development. By prioritizing refactoring as an integral part of the development process, developers can ensure that the codebase remains healthy and adaptable to change.

Another principle of effective code refactoring is to refactor with a clear understanding of the codebase and its design principles. Before embarking on a refactoring effort, developers should take the time to familiarize themselves with the existing code and its intended functionality. By understanding the purpose and structure of the code, developers can identify areas for improvement and make informed decisions about which refactoring techniques to apply. Additionally, developers should adhere to established design principles such as SOLID (Single Responsibility, Open/Closed, Liskov Substitution, Interface Segregation, Dependency Inversion) and DRY (Don't Repeat Yourself) when refactoring code. By following these principles, developers can ensure that the refactored code remains cohesive, flexible, and easy to understand.

Furthermore, effective code refactoring involves breaking down large, complex refactorings into smaller, manageable tasks. Instead of attempting to refactor an entire codebase in one go, developers should focus on refactoring one module, class, or method at a time. By breaking the refactoring process into smaller increments, developers can reduce the risk of introducing bugs and minimize the impact on ongoing development work. To break down refactorings effectively, developers can use techniques such as the "extract method," "extract class," or "extract interface" refactorings to isolate and refactor individual components of the codebase incrementally. By applying these refactorings iteratively, developers can gradually improve the overall quality of the codebase without disrupting existing functionality.

Moreover, effective code refactoring requires developers to employ automated tests to validate the correctness of their changes. Automated tests provide a safety net that allows developers to refactor code confidently without fear of introducing regressions. Before refactoring code, developers should ensure that the codebase is adequately covered by unit tests, integration tests, and acceptance tests. By running these tests regularly as part of the refactoring process, developers can detect and fix errors early, reducing the likelihood of introducing bugs during refactoring. Additionally, developers can use techniques such as test-driven development (TDD) to drive the refactoring process by writing tests for the desired behavior before making changes to the code. By leveraging automated tests, developers can refactor code with confidence, knowing that their changes are verified by a comprehensive test suite.

Furthermore, effective code refactoring involves continuous monitoring and evaluation of the refactoring effort to measure its impact and effectiveness. Developers should track metrics such as code complexity, code duplication, and test coverage before and after refactoring to assess the improvement in code quality. Additionally, developers can solicit feedback from team members and stakeholders to gather insights into the usability and maintainability of the refactored code. By collecting feedback and monitoring metrics, developers can identify areas for further improvement and iterate on the refactoring process iteratively. Additionally, developers can use tools such as static code analyzers and code review platforms to identify code smells and potential areas for refactoring automatically. By leveraging these tools, developers can streamline the refactoring process and ensure that the codebase remains clean and maintainable over time.

In summary, the principles of effective code refactoring emphasize the importance of maintaining a clean, maintainable, and adaptable codebase throughout the software development lifecycle. By refactoring early, understanding the codebase, breaking down refactorings, employing automated tests, and continuously monitoring and evaluating the refactoring effort, developers can improve the quality of their code and enhance the productivity of their development teams. By following these principles, developers can ensure that their code remains flexible, scalable, and easy to maintain, enabling them to deliver high-quality software products that meet user expectations.

Refactoring complex code bases can be a daunting task for developers, especially when dealing with large and convoluted codebases that have evolved over time. However, with the assistance of GitHub Copilot, developers can streamline the refactoring process and make it more efficient. GitHub Copilot, powered by advanced machine learning models, can analyze existing code, understand its structure and functionality, and suggest refactoring techniques to improve its quality and maintainability. Next, we explore how developers can leverage GitHub Copilot to refactor complex code bases effectively, identify common code smells and patterns, and apply refactoring techniques to enhance code readability, performance, and extensibility.

One of the primary benefits of using GitHub Copilot for refactoring complex code bases is its ability to generate accurate and contextually relevant refactoring suggestions based on the existing code. By analyzing the codebase and understanding its semantics, GitHub Copilot can provide developers with personalized refactoring recommendations tailored to the specific needs and requirements of the project. For example, developers can use GitHub Copilot to identify duplicate code segments, extract reusable methods or classes, and eliminate code smells such as long methods, deep nesting, and tight coupling. By following the suggestions provided by GitHub Copilot, developers can refactor complex code bases more efficiently and effectively, reducing the time and effort required to improve the code quality.

Moreover, GitHub Copilot can assist developers in identifying and addressing common code smells and anti-patterns that degrade the quality of the codebase. Code smells such as duplicated code, long methods, and excessive nesting can make code difficult to understand, maintain, and extend. By leveraging GitHub Copilot's code analysis capabilities, developers can detect these code smells automatically and apply appropriate refactoring techniques to eliminate them. For example, GitHub Copilot can suggest extracting methods to break down long and complex functions into smaller, more manageable units, improving code readability and maintainability. Additionally, GitHub Copilot can recommend introducing design patterns such as the Factory Method, Strategy, or Observer pattern to address specific design flaws and improve code extensibility and flexibility.

Furthermore, GitHub Copilot can help developers refactor complex code bases by suggesting alternative implementations and optimizations to improve code performance and efficiency. For example, GitHub Copilot can identify performance bottlenecks such as nested loops, inefficient algorithms, and redundant computations and propose alternative solutions to optimize code execution speed and resource utilization. Additionally, GitHub Copilot can recommend using built-in language features and libraries to streamline code and reduce its complexity. By following these suggestions, developers can refactor complex code bases to enhance performance, reduce resource consumption, and improve overall code quality.

Another advantage of using GitHub Copilot for refactoring complex code bases is its ability to assist developers in writing unit tests and validating the correctness of their refactoring changes. Unit testing is an essential practice in software development that helps ensure the reliability and stability of code by verifying its behavior under different conditions. With GitHub Copilot, developers can generate unit test scaffolding code for refactored components automatically, saving time and effort in writing test cases manually. Additionally, GitHub Copilot can provide examples of test scenarios and edge cases to cover during testing, helping developers improve the test coverage and effectiveness of their test suites. By incorporating automated testing into the refactoring process, developers can refactor complex code bases with confidence, knowing that their changes are validated by comprehensive test coverage.

Furthermore, GitHub Copilot can facilitate collaboration and knowledge sharing among developers by providing explanations and rationales for its refactoring suggestions. When suggesting refactoring techniques, GitHub Copilot can provide comments and documentation to explain the reasoning behind each suggestion and educate developers about best practices and coding conventions. Additionally, GitHub Copilot can link to relevant documentation, articles, and resources to help developers understand the underlying concepts and principles behind the suggested refactorings. By promoting knowledge sharing and collaboration, GitHub Copilot can empower developers to make informed decisions and contribute to the improvement of the codebase collectively.

In summary, GitHub Copilot offers a powerful set of tools and capabilities for refactoring complex code bases efficiently and effectively. By leveraging its advanced machine learning models, code analysis capabilities, and collaborative features, developers can streamline the refactoring process, identify and address code smells and anti-patterns, optimize code performance, and validate changes through automated testing. By incorporating GitHub Copilot into their refactoring workflows, developers can improve the quality, readability, and maintainability of their codebases, ultimately enhancing the productivity and success of their development projects.

Chapter 5: Optimizing Code Quality with Copilot

Code quality metrics and best practices play a crucial role in ensuring the reliability, maintainability, and scalability of software projects. By adhering to established coding standards and monitoring key metrics, developers can identify areas for improvement, detect potential issues early, and maintain a high level of code quality throughout the development lifecycle. Next, we explore various code quality metrics and best practices that developers can leverage to assess and improve the quality of their codebases.

One fundamental aspect of code quality is readability, which refers to the clarity and comprehensibility of code. Readable code is easier to understand, debug, and maintain, reducing the risk of errors and facilitating collaboration among team members. To measure code readability, developers can use metrics such as cyclomatic complexity, which quantifies the number of linearly independent paths through a function or method. High cyclomatic complexity values indicate complex and convoluted code that may be difficult to understand and maintain. By reducing cyclomatic complexity through refactoring and simplification, developers can improve code readability and enhance the overall quality of the codebase.

Another important aspect of code quality is maintainability, which refers to the ease with which code can be modified, extended, and updated over time. Maintainable code follows established design principles such as SOLID and DRY, which promote modularity, flexibility, and reusability. To measure code maintainability, developers can use metrics such as code duplication, which quantifies the amount of redundant code in the codebase. High levels of code duplication indicate a lack of abstraction and code reuse, which can lead to increased maintenance efforts and the risk of introducing bugs. By eliminating code duplication and adhering to design principles, developers can improve code maintainability and reduce technical debt in the codebase.

Additionally, code quality metrics can provide insights into the overall health and stability of a software project. Metrics such as code coverage, which measures the percentage of code covered by automated tests, can help developers assess the effectiveness of their testing efforts and identify areas of the codebase that require additional testing. High code coverage values indicate a comprehensive test suite that adequately validates the behavior of the code under different conditions. By increasing code coverage and writing more robust tests, developers can improve the reliability and stability of their codebase, reducing the likelihood of encountering bugs and regressions in production.

Furthermore, code quality metrics can help developers identify potential security vulnerabilities and compliance issues in their codebase. Metrics such as code complexity and dependency analysis can highlight areas of the codebase that may be susceptible to security exploits or violations of regulatory standards. For example, high levels of code complexity in authentication or encryption algorithms may increase the risk of security vulnerabilities, while outdated or vulnerable dependencies may expose the project to known security risks. By conducting regular security audits and addressing identified issues promptly, developers can enhance the security and compliance posture of their codebase, mitigating the risk of security breaches and legal liabilities.

Moreover, code quality metrics can facilitate continuous improvement and optimization of the development process. By tracking metrics such as code churn, which measures the frequency of code changes, and code review turnaround time, which measures the speed at which code reviews are completed, developers can identify bottlenecks and inefficiencies in the development workflow. For example, high code churn rates may indicate instability or poor planning in the development process, while long code review turnaround times may indicate a lack of communication or collaboration among team members. By addressing these issues and optimizing the development process iteratively, developers can improve productivity, reduce time to market, and deliver higher-quality software products.

In summary, code quality metrics and best practices are essential tools for assessing, monitoring, and improving the quality of software projects. By measuring key aspects of code quality such as readability, maintainability, reliability, and security, developers can identify areas for improvement and prioritize efforts to address them effectively. By incorporating code quality metrics into their development workflow and adhering to established best practices, developers can maintain a high level of code quality, reduce technical debt, and build more robust and scalable software solutions.

Leveraging Copilot suggestions for code quality improvement is a valuable strategy that developers can employ to enhance the overall quality and maintainability of their codebases. GitHub Copilot, powered by advanced machine learning models, provides intelligent code suggestions and completions based on the context of the code being written, enabling developers to write cleaner, more efficient code with fewer errors and inconsistencies. Next, we explore how developers can leverage Copilot suggestions effectively to improve code quality, identify common code smells and anti-patterns, and enforce coding standards and best practices.

One of the primary benefits of leveraging Copilot suggestions is its ability to assist developers in writing code that adheres to established coding standards and best practices. By analyzing the context of the code and understanding the developer's intent, Copilot can provide suggestions that align with industry-standard coding conventions, naming conventions, and style guidelines. For example, when writing a function or method, Copilot can suggest appropriate parameter names, variable names, and function signatures that follow naming conventions such as camelCase or snake_case. By following these suggestions, developers can ensure consistency and readability across their codebase, making it easier to understand and maintain.

Moreover, Copilot can help developers identify and address common code smells and anti-patterns that degrade the quality of the codebase. Code smells such as duplicated code, long methods, and excessive nesting can make code difficult to understand, debug, and maintain. By analyzing the context of the code and comparing it to known patterns and best practices, Copilot can suggest refactorings and optimizations to eliminate code smells and improve code quality. For example, Copilot can suggest extracting methods to break down long and complex functions into smaller, more manageable units, or suggest replacing nested loops with more efficient algorithms. By following these suggestions, developers can refactor their code to improve readability, maintainability, and performance.

Additionally, Copilot can assist developers in writing more robust and reliable code by suggesting error handling techniques and defensive programming practices. For example, when working with file I/O operations or network requests, Copilot can suggest adding error handling code to gracefully handle exceptions and failures. By incorporating error handling code into their applications, developers can improve the resilience and fault tolerance of their software, reducing the risk of crashes and unexpected behavior in production. Furthermore, Copilot can suggest unit tests and test cases to validate the correctness and functionality of the code, helping developers catch bugs and regressions early in the development process.

Furthermore, Copilot can aid developers in adopting modern software engineering practices such as test-driven development (TDD) and behavior-driven development (BDD). By providing examples of test scenarios and test cases, Copilot can guide developers in writing tests before implementing the corresponding functionality, enabling them to design more modular, testable, and maintainable code. For example, when writing a new feature or fixing a bug, Copilot can suggest writing unit tests or integration tests to verify the expected behavior of the code. By following a test-driven approach, developers can improve the overall quality of their codebase and reduce the likelihood of introducing bugs and regressions.

Moreover, Copilot can facilitate code reviews and collaboration among team members by providing explanations and context for its suggestions. When reviewing code changes, developers can use Copilot to suggest alternative implementations, point out potential issues or improvements, and provide feedback on coding style and best practices. By leveraging Copilot's suggestions and insights, developers can engage in constructive discussions and make informed decisions about code changes, leading to higher-quality code and more effective collaboration. Additionally, Copilot can help onboard new team members by providing explanations and examples of common coding patterns and idioms used in the codebase, enabling them to ramp up quickly and contribute effectively to the project.

In summary, leveraging Copilot suggestions for code quality improvement is a valuable strategy that developers can use to enhance the quality, readability, and maintainability of their codebases. By analyzing the context of the code and providing intelligent suggestions based on industry-standard coding conventions, best practices, and design patterns, Copilot can help developers write cleaner, more efficient code with fewer errors and inconsistencies. By incorporating Copilot into their development workflow and collaborating with team members, developers can improve the overall quality of their codebase, reduce technical debt, and deliver more reliable and scalable software solutions.

Chapter 6: Enhancing Collaboration through Copilot Suggestions

Facilitating team collaboration with Copilot is an essential aspect of modern software development practices. As teams work together to build complex software solutions, effective collaboration tools and techniques become increasingly crucial for ensuring productivity, efficiency, and cohesion among team members. GitHub Copilot, with its intelligent code suggestions and completions, offers valuable features and capabilities that can streamline collaboration workflows, foster knowledge sharing, and enhance teamwork dynamics. Next, we explore how developers can leverage Copilot to facilitate team collaboration effectively, improve communication, and accelerate the development process.

One way Copilot facilitates team collaboration is by providing real-time code suggestions and completions that help developers write code more efficiently and consistently. As team members collaborate on coding tasks, Copilot can assist them by suggesting relevant code snippets, functions, and algorithms based on the context of the code being written. For example, when a developer is implementing a specific feature or fixing a bug, Copilot can suggest relevant code patterns, best practices, and design patterns to guide them in their coding efforts. By providing intelligent code suggestions, Copilot helps ensure consistency and alignment with established coding standards and conventions across the team's codebase.

Moreover, Copilot can serve as a valuable learning tool for team members by providing explanations and examples of coding concepts, techniques, and patterns. As developers interact with Copilot's suggestions, they can gain insights into different approaches to problem-solving, learn new programming languages or frameworks, and discover best practices and design patterns used in software development. For example, when a developer encounters a complex coding problem, they can rely on Copilot to provide alternative solutions and explanations of the underlying principles and trade-offs involved. By leveraging Copilot as a learning resource, team members can expand their knowledge and skills, fostering a culture of continuous learning and improvement within the team.

Furthermore, Copilot can facilitate code reviews and peer feedback by providing contextual suggestions and insights during the review process. As team members review each other's code changes, they can use Copilot to suggest alternative implementations, point out potential issues or improvements, and provide feedback on coding style and best practices. For example, when reviewing a pull request, a team member can use Copilot to suggest refactorings, optimizations, or bug fixes that improve the quality and maintainability of the code. By incorporating Copilot into the code review workflow, teams can ensure that code changes are thoroughly reviewed, discussed, and refined before being merged into the main codebase.

Additionally, Copilot can aid in the onboarding process for new team members by providing explanations and examples of common coding patterns and idioms used in the codebase. As new developers join the team, they can leverage Copilot to familiarize themselves with the codebase, understand the project structure and architecture, and learn about the team's coding conventions and best practices. For example, when exploring the codebase for the first time, a new developer can use Copilot to search for relevant code snippets, examples, or documentation that help them understand how different components of the system interact and collaborate. By providing guidance and context, Copilot accelerates the onboarding process and enables new team members to become productive contributors more quickly.

Furthermore, Copilot can enhance collaboration among distributed or remote teams by providing a shared understanding of the codebase and enabling asynchronous communication. As team members work across different time zones or locations, Copilot serves as a virtual assistant that provides consistent and reliable support, regardless of geographical constraints. For example, when a team member encounters a coding problem outside of regular working hours, they can rely on Copilot to provide assistance and guidance, reducing the need for synchronous communication and enabling team members to work autonomously and efficiently. By fostering asynchronous collaboration and providing access to a shared knowledge base, Copilot empowers distributed teams to collaborate effectively and deliver high-quality software solutions.

In summary, facilitating team collaboration with Copilot is essential for modern software development teams seeking to enhance productivity, efficiency, and cohesion. By providing intelligent code suggestions, fostering learning and knowledge sharing, facilitating code reviews and feedback, aiding in the onboarding process for new team members, and supporting distributed collaboration, Copilot enables teams to work more effectively together and deliver high-quality software solutions. By incorporating Copilot into their collaboration workflows and leveraging its capabilities to streamline communication and coordination, teams can achieve greater agility, innovation, and success in their software development endeavors.

Using Copilot suggestions for pair programming is a strategic approach to leverage the power of artificial intelligence in collaborative coding sessions. Pair programming, a widely adopted agile software development practice, involves two programmers working together on the same code at the same time. It offers numerous benefits, including improved code quality, knowledge sharing, and problem-solving efficiency. With the introduction of GitHub Copilot, developers now have access to an advanced AI-powered tool that can generate code suggestions in real-time based on the context of the code being written. Incorporating Copilot suggestions into pair programming sessions can enhance collaboration, increase productivity, and facilitate code exploration and experimentation.

To start using Copilot suggestions for pair programming, developers can initiate a collaborative coding session with their partner using a supported integrated development environment (IDE) such as Visual Studio Code. Once the session is underway, both programmers can begin writing code together, with one developer actively typing while the other provides guidance, feedback, and support. As they work together, they can leverage Copilot suggestions to accelerate their coding tasks, explore different implementation options, and overcome coding challenges more effectively.

One way to utilize Copilot suggestions in pair programming is to use them as a source of inspiration and guidance when tackling complex coding problems. When encountering a particularly challenging task or unfamiliar coding pattern, developers can consult Copilot for alternative solutions, code snippets, and implementation ideas. By integrating Copilot suggestions into their problem-solving process, developers can broaden their perspective, explore different approaches, and discover new ways to address the problem at hand.

Furthermore, Copilot suggestions can serve as a valuable learning resource for both programmers involved in the pair programming session. As they collaborate on coding tasks, developers can analyze and discuss the suggestions provided by Copilot, examine the underlying logic and algorithms, and gain insights into best practices and coding conventions. This collaborative learning experience not only enhances the individual skills of each developer but also strengthens their collective expertise as a pair programming team.

Moreover, Copilot suggestions can facilitate code exploration and experimentation during pair programming sessions. As developers collaborate on implementing a new feature or resolving a bug, they can use Copilot to generate code snippets that illustrate different implementation approaches or demonstrate specific coding techniques. By experimenting with various code suggestions, developers can iteratively refine their solution, evaluate different design choices, and ultimately arrive at a more robust and efficient implementation.

Additionally, Copilot suggestions can aid in code review and feedback processes within the pair programming session. As developers write code together, they can use Copilot to suggest improvements, optimizations, or refactorings to their partner's code in real-time. This immediate feedback loop enables developers to continuously review and refine their code as they write it, leading to higher code quality and fewer errors.

Furthermore, Copilot suggestions can help maintain consistency and adherence to coding standards and best practices within the pair programming session. As developers collaborate on writing code, Copilot can provide suggestions that align with established coding conventions, style guides, and project-specific requirements. By following Copilot's recommendations, developers can ensure that their code remains consistent, readable, and maintainable throughout the development process.

Moreover, Copilot suggestions can promote knowledge sharing and skill development within the pair programming team. As developers collaborate on coding tasks, they can discuss the suggestions provided by Copilot, share insights, and exchange ideas about coding techniques, algorithms, and design patterns. This collaborative learning experience fosters a culture of continuous improvement and enables developers to expand their knowledge and expertise in software development.

Additionally, Copilot suggestions can enhance the productivity of pair programming sessions by automating repetitive coding tasks and reducing cognitive load. As developers work together on writing code, Copilot can generate boilerplate code, common utility functions, and other repetitive constructs, allowing developers to focus on more challenging and creative aspects of the coding task. By offloading routine coding tasks to Copilot, developers can work more efficiently and effectively as a pair programming team.

In summary, using Copilot suggestions for pair programming is a powerful approach to enhance collaboration, increase productivity, and improve code quality in software development teams. By leveraging Copilot's AI-powered code generation capabilities, developers can explore new coding techniques, experiment with different implementation approaches, and receive immediate feedback and guidance during pair programming sessions. Incorporating Copilot into pair programming workflows enables developers to work more effectively together, share knowledge and expertise, and deliver high-quality software solutions more efficiently.

Chapter 7: Streamlining Development Workflows with Copilot

Integrating Copilot into existing development workflows is a strategic endeavor aimed at enhancing productivity, code quality, and collaboration within software development teams. Copilot, an AI-powered code generation tool developed by GitHub, offers a range of features and capabilities designed to streamline the coding process and provide valuable assistance to developers. By seamlessly integrating Copilot into their existing workflows, development teams can leverage its advanced capabilities to accelerate development cycles, improve code consistency, and foster collaboration among team members.

The first step in integrating Copilot into existing development workflows is to ensure that all team members are familiar with its features and functionalities. This may involve providing training sessions or tutorials to familiarize developers with how Copilot works and how it can be used to enhance their coding process. Additionally, it is essential to establish clear guidelines and best practices for using Copilot effectively within the team, ensuring that everyone understands how to leverage its capabilities to their full potential.

Once developers are acquainted with Copilot, the next step is to seamlessly integrate it into the team's existing development tools and processes. This may involve integrating Copilot directly into the team's preferred integrated development environment (IDE), such as Visual Studio Code or JetBrains IntelliJ IDEA. GitHub provides plugins and extensions for popular IDEs that enable developers to access Copilot's features directly within their coding environment, allowing for a seamless and frictionless integration experience.

Furthermore, integrating Copilot into existing version control systems, such as Git, is essential for ensuring smooth collaboration and versioning of code changes within the team. By integrating Copilot with Git, developers can easily commit and push code changes to their repositories, collaborate with team members on code reviews, and seamlessly merge changes into the main codebase. GitHub provides native integrations with Git, allowing developers to interact with their repositories directly from within their IDEs or through the command line.

In addition to IDE and version control system integrations, integrating Copilot into existing project management and collaboration tools can further enhance team productivity and communication. For example, teams can integrate Copilot with project management platforms like Jira or Trello to streamline task management and issue tracking processes. By linking Copilot-generated code snippets to specific tasks or user stories, teams can ensure that all code changes are aligned with project requirements and priorities.

Moreover, integrating Copilot into continuous integration and continuous deployment (CI/CD) pipelines can automate code testing, validation, and deployment processes, further streamlining the development workflow. Teams can leverage Copilot-generated code to automate repetitive tasks, such as writing unit tests, generating documentation, or configuring deployment pipelines. By integrating Copilot with CI/CD tools like Jenkins, CircleCI, or GitHub Actions, teams can ensure that code changes are thoroughly tested and deployed to production environments with minimal manual intervention.

Another critical aspect of integrating Copilot into existing development workflows is to establish clear communication channels and collaboration practices within the team. By fostering open communication and collaboration, teams can effectively leverage Copilot's features to share knowledge, exchange ideas, and collectively solve coding challenges. This may involve regular code reviews, pair programming sessions, or team meetings to discuss Copilot-generated code suggestions and ensure alignment with project goals and coding standards.

Furthermore, integrating Copilot into existing code review processes can improve code quality and facilitate knowledge sharing among team members. By incorporating Copilot-generated code snippets into code reviews, teams can identify potential issues, discuss alternative implementation approaches, and provide feedback to ensure that code changes meet quality standards and best practices. This collaborative code review process helps spread knowledge and expertise across the team and fosters a culture of continuous improvement and learning.

In summary, integrating Copilot into existing development workflows offers numerous benefits for software development teams, including increased productivity, improved code quality, and enhanced collaboration. By seamlessly integrating Copilot into IDEs, version control systems, project management tools, and CI/CD pipelines, teams can leverage its advanced capabilities to streamline development processes, automate repetitive tasks, and foster collaboration among team members. Additionally, establishing clear communication channels and collaboration practices within the team is essential for effectively leveraging Copilot's features and maximizing its impact on team productivity and code quality.

Customizing Copilot for seamless workflow integration is a crucial aspect of leveraging its capabilities effectively within the development process. Copilot, with its AI-powered code generation features, offers developers the flexibility to tailor its behavior and preferences to suit their specific workflow requirements. By customizing Copilot, developers can optimize their coding experience, improve productivity, and ensure smooth integration with existing tools and processes.

One of the key customization options available to developers is the ability to configure Copilot's code generation preferences and suggestions. Copilot allows developers to adjust various settings, such as the preferred programming language, code style preferences, and code snippet length. These preferences can be configured directly within the IDE using the Copilot plugin or extension settings, allowing developers to tailor Copilot's suggestions to match their coding style and project requirements.

For example, developers can specify their preferred programming language using the copilot language command in the terminal. This command allows developers to set the primary programming language for Copilot to use when generating code suggestions. By specifying the desired language, developers can ensure that Copilot provides relevant and accurate code suggestions that align with the project's technology stack.

In addition to language preferences, developers can customize Copilot's behavior and suggestions by adjusting various settings related to code complexity, code quality, and context awareness. For instance, developers can use the copilot complexity command to adjust Copilot's sensitivity to code complexity levels. By specifying a desired complexity threshold, developers can control the level of detail and sophistication in Copilot's code suggestions, ensuring that they align with the project's requirements and development goals.

Moreover, developers can customize Copilot's suggestions by providing feedback on the quality and relevance of generated code snippets. Copilot allows developers to rate individual suggestions using simple commands or keyboard shortcuts, such as thumbs-up or thumbs-down. This feedback mechanism helps Copilot learn from developers' preferences and adapt its suggestions over time, improving the accuracy and relevance of future code suggestions.

Another important aspect of customizing Copilot is the ability to integrate it with existing codebases, libraries, and frameworks used in the project. Copilot allows developers to specify custom code templates, snippets, or boilerplate code that can be reused across multiple files or projects. By defining these custom templates, developers can streamline common coding tasks and ensure consistency in code structure and formatting.

For example, developers can use the copilot template command to define custom code templates for specific use cases, such as creating new classes, functions, or data structures. These templates can include placeholders for variable names, function parameters, or other dynamic elements, allowing developers to quickly generate code snippets that adhere to project conventions and standards.

Furthermore, developers can leverage Copilot's integration with version control systems, such as Git, to customize its behavior based on project-specific requirements and constraints. Copilot allows developers to specify project-specific settings and preferences using configuration files or metadata stored within the repository. By defining these project-specific settings, developers can ensure consistent behavior and preferences across team members and development environments.

Additionally, developers can customize Copilot's behavior by integrating it with other development tools and services commonly used in the project. For instance, developers can use the copilot integrate command to connect Copilot with project management tools, issue trackers, or communication platforms. This integration allows Copilot to access additional context and information about the project, enabling more intelligent code suggestions and assistance.

In summary, customizing Copilot for seamless workflow integration is essential for maximizing its effectiveness and utility within the development process. By adjusting Copilot's code generation preferences, integrating it with existing tools and processes, and providing feedback on generated code suggestions, developers can tailor Copilot to meet their specific workflow requirements and coding preferences. This customization empowers developers to optimize their coding experience, improve productivity, and deliver high-quality code more efficiently.

Chapter 8: Handling Complex Projects with Copilot Assistance

Managing complexity is a crucial aspect of software development, and leveraging tools like Copilot can greatly assist in this endeavor. Copilot, with its AI-powered code generation capabilities, offers developers various strategies to handle complexity effectively and maintain codebases efficiently. These strategies encompass a range of techniques, from simplifying code logic to modularizing complex systems, all aimed at reducing cognitive load, improving maintainability, and enhancing overall code quality.

One strategy for managing complexity with Copilot is to break down complex tasks into smaller, more manageable units. This can be achieved by decomposing large functions or methods into smaller, more focused ones, each responsible for a specific task or functionality. Copilot can assist in this process by providing suggestions for extracting and refactoring code blocks into separate functions or modules, thereby simplifying the overall code structure and reducing complexity.

For example, when faced with a complex algorithm or business logic, developers can use Copilot to generate helper functions or utility methods that encapsulate specific subtasks. By decomposing the problem into smaller, more digestible units, developers can better understand and reason about the code, making it easier to maintain and extend over time. Additionally, modularizing complex systems can also facilitate code reuse and improve overall code organization.

Another strategy for managing complexity with Copilot is to leverage design patterns and architectural principles to structure code in a more modular and maintainable way. Copilot can provide suggestions for implementing common design patterns, such as the Singleton pattern, Factory pattern, or Observer pattern, based on the context and requirements of the project. By adhering to established design principles, developers can create code that is more flexible, extensible, and easier to comprehend.

For instance, when working on a project that requires object creation with a single, globally accessible instance, developers can use Copilot to generate code for implementing the Singleton pattern. This pattern ensures that only one instance of a class is created and provides a global point of access to that instance. By following this pattern, developers can simplify object management and ensure consistent behavior throughout the application.

Moreover, Copilot can assist in managing complexity by suggesting alternative approaches or refactorings to simplify code logic and reduce redundancy. For example, when encountering nested conditional statements or complex control flow, developers can use Copilot to generate alternative implementations using techniques such as early returns, guard clauses, or switch statements. These refactorings can help streamline code logic, improve readability, and reduce the cognitive burden of understanding complex branching structures.

Additionally, Copilot can help manage complexity by providing suggestions for error handling and exception management. When dealing with error-prone code or critical sections that require robust error handling, developers can use Copilot to generate boilerplate code for implementing try-catch blocks, error propagation mechanisms, or custom exception classes. By handling errors gracefully and consistently, developers can improve the reliability and robustness of their codebases.

Furthermore, Copilot can assist in managing complexity by automating repetitive tasks and reducing the need for manual intervention. For example, when working with large datasets or complex data processing pipelines, developers can use Copilot to generate code for common data manipulation tasks, such as filtering, sorting, or transforming data. By automating these routine tasks, developers can focus on higher-level problem-solving and innovation, rather than getting bogged down in low-level implementation details.

In summary, managing complexity with Copilot involves leveraging its AI-powered code generation capabilities to simplify code logic, modularize complex systems, and adhere to established design principles. By breaking down complex tasks into smaller units, leveraging design patterns, and automating repetitive tasks, developers can reduce cognitive load, improve maintainability, and enhance overall code quality. By incorporating these strategies into their development workflow, developers can effectively manage complexity and build robust, maintainable software systems.

Managing complex project architectures is a daunting task for developers, requiring meticulous planning, thoughtful design, and efficient implementation. With the advent of GitHub Copilot, developers now have a powerful ally in navigating the intricacies of complex project architectures. Copilot offers a myriad of solutions and strategies tailored to address the unique challenges posed by complex project structures, enabling developers to streamline development workflows, enhance code maintainability, and improve overall project scalability.

One of the key challenges in managing complex project architectures is ensuring consistency and coherence across different components and modules. Copilot excels in this regard by providing intelligent code suggestions that adhere to established design patterns and architectural principles. For instance, when designing a microservices-based architecture, Copilot can offer guidance on structuring services, implementing communication protocols, and handling cross-cutting concerns such as authentication, logging, and error handling. By leveraging Copilot's expertise, developers can build scalable and resilient microservices architectures that meet the requirements of modern, cloud-native applications.

In addition to providing architectural guidance, Copilot can also assist in automating repetitive tasks and boilerplate code generation, thereby reducing development overhead and accelerating time-to-market. For instance, when working with frameworks such as Spring Boot or Django, Copilot can generate scaffolding code for creating RESTful APIs, defining database models, and configuring middleware components. By automating these routine tasks, developers can focus on implementing business logic and delivering value to end-users, rather than getting bogged down in low-level implementation details.

Moreover, Copilot can help in managing dependencies and versioning issues, which are common challenges in complex project architectures. By analyzing codebases and understanding the context of the project, Copilot can suggest appropriate libraries, frameworks, and tools to address specific requirements and constraints. For example, when building a data-intensive application, Copilot can recommend libraries for data serialization, caching, and distributed computing, helping developers make informed decisions and avoid compatibility issues.

Another area where Copilot shines is in facilitating collaboration and knowledge sharing among team members. By providing context-aware code suggestions and documentation snippets, Copilot enables developers to onboard new team members quickly, share best practices, and maintain consistent coding standards across the project. Additionally, Copilot's collaborative coding features, such as shared workspaces and real-time editing, foster teamwork and communication, enabling developers to collaborate effectively on complex tasks and resolve issues efficiently.

Furthermore, Copilot can assist in optimizing project architectures for performance, scalability, and reliability. By analyzing code patterns and identifying performance bottlenecks, Copilot can suggest optimizations and refactorings to improve code efficiency and resource utilization. For instance, when working on a high-traffic web application, Copilot can recommend caching strategies, load balancing techniques, and asynchronous processing patterns to enhance scalability and responsiveness.

In summary, Copilot offers a comprehensive set of solutions for managing complex project architectures, spanning architectural design, code generation, dependency management, collaboration, and optimization. By leveraging Copilot's AI-powered capabilities, developers can navigate the complexities of modern software development with confidence, delivering robust, scalable, and maintainable solutions that meet the evolving needs of their organizations and users. As the field of software engineering continues to evolve, Copilot remains an invaluable tool for developers seeking to tackle the challenges of complexity and deliver innovative solutions that drive business success.

Chapter 9: Mastering Code Review Processes with Copilot

Code review is an indispensable aspect of the software development lifecycle, ensuring code quality, adherence to coding standards, and knowledge sharing among team members. Traditionally, code reviews are conducted manually, requiring developers to inspect code changes line by line and provide feedback. However, this process can be time-consuming and error-prone, especially for large codebases or distributed teams. Leveraging GitHub Copilot for code review automation offers a promising solution to these challenges, streamlining the review process, improving code quality, and enhancing developer productivity.

One of the key benefits of using Copilot for code review automation is its ability to generate contextual code suggestions based on the code being reviewed. Instead of manually identifying issues or potential improvements, developers can rely on Copilot to offer insightful recommendations and best practices directly within the code review interface. For example, when reviewing a pull request that introduces a new feature or fixes a bug, Copilot can suggest alternative implementations, point out potential edge cases, or provide explanations for complex code segments, helping reviewers make informed decisions and provide constructive feedback.

To integrate Copilot into the code review workflow, developers can utilize GitHub's pull request review features, such as code comments and inline suggestions. When reviewing a pull request, reviewers can invoke Copilot using the "@copilot" command within a code comment, prompting Copilot to analyze the code changes and provide relevant suggestions. For instance, if a reviewer notices a suboptimal algorithm or a redundant code snippet, they can request Copilot's assistance by mentioning "@copilot" followed by a description of the issue. Copilot will then analyze the surrounding code context and offer suggestions for improvement, which can be further discussed and validated by the review team.

Furthermore, Copilot can assist in enforcing coding standards and best practices during the review process. By analyzing the code changes against predefined style guides or project-specific rules, Copilot can identify deviations from established conventions and provide recommendations for alignment. For example, if a pull request introduces inconsistent variable naming or incorrect usage of language features, Copilot can flag these issues and suggest corrective actions, ensuring code consistency and maintainability across the project.

In addition to facilitating code reviews, Copilot can also contribute to knowledge sharing and skill development within the development team. By providing explanatory comments and code snippets, Copilot helps developers understand complex concepts, idiomatic patterns, and domain-specific techniques, fostering a culture of continuous learning and improvement. For junior developers or team members new to a codebase, Copilot's insights can serve as valuable learning resources, accelerating their onboarding process and enhancing their coding proficiency over time.

To maximize the effectiveness of Copilot for code review automation, it's essential to establish clear guidelines and expectations for its usage within the team. While Copilot can offer valuable suggestions and insights, it's important to remember that it's not a substitute for human judgment or domain expertise. Developers should critically evaluate Copilot's suggestions in the context of the specific project requirements, considering factors such as performance, security, and maintainability. Additionally, teams should continuously monitor and refine their Copilot usage to ensure that it aligns with evolving coding standards and best practices.

Overall, leveraging Copilot for code review automation offers numerous benefits for development teams, including streamlined review processes, improved code quality, and enhanced knowledge sharing. By integrating Copilot into the code review workflow and establishing clear guidelines for its usage, teams can harness the power of AI to drive efficiency, consistency, and collaboration in their software development efforts. As Copilot continues to evolve and improve, it promises to revolutionize the way developers approach code reviews, enabling them to deliver higher-quality software more effectively and efficiently than ever before.

Code review is a crucial aspect of software development, ensuring code quality, adherence to standards, and knowledge sharing among team members. Traditionally, code reviews are conducted manually, requiring developers to scrutinize changes line by line. However, with the advent of AI-powered tools like GitHub Copilot, code review processes can be significantly enhanced. Implementing effective code review strategies with Copilot involves leveraging its capabilities to streamline the review process, improve code quality, and foster collaboration within development teams.

One of the primary advantages of integrating Copilot into code review workflows is its ability to provide contextual code suggestions based on the code being reviewed. Instead of relying solely on manual inspection, developers can utilize Copilot to offer insights and recommendations directly within the review interface. For instance, when reviewing a pull request, developers can invoke Copilot using the "@copilot" command within a code comment to solicit suggestions for improving code quality or addressing specific issues.

To deploy Copilot for code review, developers can follow a straightforward process. After creating a pull request in their version control system, such as Git, they can navigate to the code review interface on the hosting platform, such as GitHub or GitLab. Within the review interface, developers can access the comment section and invoke Copilot using the designated command, such as "@copilot suggest" or "@copilot review." Copilot will then analyze the code changes and provide relevant suggestions, which can be reviewed and discussed by the team.

Furthermore, Copilot can assist in enforcing coding standards and best practices during code reviews. By analyzing code changes against predefined style guides or project-specific rules, Copilot can identify deviations and provide recommendations for alignment. For example, if a pull request introduces inconsistent formatting or violates naming conventions, Copilot can flag these issues and suggest corrective actions, ensuring code consistency across the project.

In addition to offering suggestions for code improvements, Copilot can also contribute to knowledge sharing and skill development within the team. By providing explanatory comments and code snippets, Copilot helps developers understand complex concepts and idiomatic patterns. This fosters a culture of continuous learning and improvement, empowering team members to enhance their coding proficiency over time.

To maximize the effectiveness of Copilot for code review, it's essential to establish clear guidelines and expectations for its usage within the team. While Copilot can offer valuable insights, it's important to remember that it's not a substitute for human judgment or domain expertise. Developers should critically evaluate Copilot's suggestions in the context of the project requirements, considering factors such as performance, security, and maintainability.

Moreover, teams should regularly review and refine their Copilot usage to ensure that it aligns with evolving coding standards and best practices. By incorporating feedback from code reviews and monitoring the impact of Copilot suggestions on code quality, teams can continuously improve their review processes and leverage Copilot to its full potential.

In summary, implementing effective code review strategies with Copilot offers numerous benefits for development teams, including streamlined review processes, improved code quality, and enhanced collaboration. By integrating Copilot into the code review workflow and establishing clear guidelines for its usage, teams can harness the power of AI to drive efficiency and consistency in their software development efforts. As Copilot continues to evolve and improve, it holds the promise of revolutionizing the way developers approach code reviews, ultimately leading to the delivery of higher-quality software products.

Chapter 10: Harnessing Copilot for Project Management

Using GitHub Copilot for project planning and scheduling can significantly streamline the process of organizing and managing software development projects. Copilot's AI capabilities can assist in various aspects of project planning, from creating task lists and estimating project timelines to generating code snippets for specific features. By leveraging Copilot effectively, teams can enhance productivity, improve communication, and ensure the successful delivery of projects on time and within budget.

One of the key features of Copilot that facilitates project planning is its ability to generate code snippets based on natural language descriptions. This functionality can be particularly useful during the initial phase of project planning when defining project requirements and breaking down tasks. Developers can use Copilot to describe the desired functionality or features in plain language, and Copilot can generate corresponding code snippets or suggest relevant libraries and frameworks.

To utilize Copilot for project planning, developers can interact with the tool directly within their integrated development environment (IDE) or text editor. For instance, in Visual Studio Code, developers can install the Copilot extension and enable it to provide suggestions as they write code or comments. When planning a project, developers can create a new file or document for outlining project requirements, milestones, and tasks. As they describe each task or feature, they can invoke Copilot using keyboard shortcuts or commands, such as "Ctrl+Space" or "@copilot suggest."

Copilot will then analyze the input text and offer suggestions for code snippets or relevant resources based on the context provided. For example, if a developer describes a feature requirement in natural language, such as "implement user authentication using JWT tokens," Copilot can generate code snippets for implementing JWT-based authentication in the preferred programming language.

In addition to generating code snippets, Copilot can also assist in estimating project timelines and resource allocation. By analyzing historical data and patterns from open-source repositories, Copilot can provide insights into the complexity and effort required for implementing specific features or tasks. Developers can leverage this information to create realistic project schedules and allocate resources effectively.

Moreover, Copilot can facilitate collaboration and communication among team members during the project planning phase. By providing suggestions and automating repetitive tasks, Copilot allows developers to focus on higher-level planning and decision-making. Team members can review and refine Copilot's suggestions collaboratively, ensuring alignment with project goals and objectives.

Furthermore, Copilot can help identify potential risks and dependencies early in the project planning process.

By analyzing code patterns and detecting common pitfalls, Copilot can alert developers to potential challenges or roadblocks before they arise. This proactive approach enables teams to mitigate risks and plan accordingly, minimizing disruptions to the project timeline.

To ensure effective use of Copilot for project planning, teams should establish clear guidelines and workflows for incorporating Copilot into the planning process. Developers should be trained on how to interact with Copilot and interpret its suggestions accurately. Additionally, teams should regularly review and refine their project plans based on feedback and insights gathered from Copilot.

In summary, using GitHub Copilot for project planning and scheduling offers numerous benefits for software development teams, including improved productivity, better resource allocation, and enhanced collaboration. By leveraging Copilot's AI capabilities to generate code snippets, estimate project timelines, and identify risks, teams can streamline the planning process and increase the likelihood of project success. As Copilot continues to evolve and improve, it holds great potential for revolutionizing project planning practices in software development.

Managing project resources is a critical aspect of project management, and integrating GitHub Copilot into resource management processes can significantly enhance efficiency and productivity. Copilot's AI capabilities can assist in various resource management tasks, including resource allocation, task assignment, and tracking resource utilization. By leveraging Copilot effectively, project managers can streamline resource management workflows, optimize resource utilization, and ensure the successful delivery of projects within budget constraints.

One of the key challenges in project resource management is effectively allocating resources to tasks based on project requirements and priorities. Copilot can aid in this process by analyzing project requirements and providing suggestions for resource allocation based on historical data and patterns. Project managers can interact with Copilot within their preferred IDE or text editor to review and refine resource allocation plans. For example, they can use commands such as "@copilot suggest" to generate resource allocation recommendations based on project specifications.

Furthermore, Copilot can assist in task assignment by generating code snippets or providing recommendations for specific tasks based on developers' skill sets and availability. Project managers can use Copilot to identify suitable team members for each task and assign responsibilities accordingly. This helps ensure that tasks are assigned to individuals with the necessary expertise and availability to complete them efficiently.

In addition to resource allocation and task assignment, Copilot can also help track resource utilization throughout the project lifecycle. By analyzing code contributions and commit history, Copilot can provide insights into individual developers' contributions and identify potential bottlenecks or resource constraints. Project managers can use this information to reallocate resources as needed to maintain project progress and meet deadlines.

Moreover, Copilot can assist in identifying potential resource conflicts or dependencies early in the project lifecycle. By analyzing code dependencies and detecting overlapping tasks, Copilot can alert project managers to potential resource conflicts before they impact project progress. Project managers can then take proactive measures to resolve conflicts and ensure smooth project execution.

To effectively manage project resources with Copilot integration, project managers should establish clear guidelines and workflows for incorporating Copilot into resource management processes. They should ensure that team members are trained on how to interact with Copilot and interpret its suggestions accurately. Additionally, project managers should regularly review resource allocation plans and adjust them as needed based on project requirements and constraints.

Furthermore, project managers can use Copilot to automate repetitive resource management tasks, such as scheduling meetings or updating resource allocation spreadsheets. By automating these tasks, project managers can free up time to focus on higher-level strategic planning and decision-making.

Overall, integrating GitHub Copilot into project resource management processes offers numerous benefits for project managers and development teams. By leveraging Copilot's AI capabilities to assist in resource allocation, task assignment, and resource utilization tracking, project managers can streamline resource management workflows, optimize resource utilization, and ensure project success. As Copilot continues to evolve and improve, it holds great potential for revolutionizing project resource management practices in software development projects.

BOOK 4
EXPERT INSIGHTS
LEVERAGING GITHUB COPILOT FOR COMPLEX
DEVELOPMENT TASKS

ROB BOTWRIGHT

Chapter 1: Understanding Complex Development Challenges

Identifying key challenges in modern software development is crucial for understanding the landscape in which developers operate and for devising effective strategies to address them. In today's fast-paced and ever-evolving technological environment, software development faces numerous complexities and hurdles that developers must navigate to deliver high-quality products on time and within budget.

One prominent challenge in modern software development is the rapid pace of technological change. As new technologies emerge and existing ones evolve, developers must constantly adapt to stay abreast of the latest trends and tools. This requires continuous learning and upskilling, which can be time-consuming and challenging, particularly for developers with limited resources or competing priorities. To mitigate this challenge, developers can leverage online resources, participate in training programs, and engage with the developer community to stay informed about new developments in technology.

Another significant challenge is the increasing complexity of software systems. As software applications become more sophisticated and interconnected, managing their complexity becomes increasingly difficult. Developers must contend with large codebases, intricate architectural designs, and intricate dependencies, which can lead to issues such as code duplication, tight coupling, and scalability problems. To address this challenge, developers can adopt software engineering best practices such as modular design, design patterns, and code refactoring to break down complex systems into smaller, more manageable components.

Furthermore, software development teams often face challenges related to collaboration and communication. In today's globalized and distributed work environment, teams may be geographically dispersed, making effective communication and collaboration more challenging. Additionally, differences in time zones, cultural norms, and communication styles can further complicate collaboration efforts. To overcome these challenges, teams can leverage collaboration tools such as version control systems, issue trackers, and project management platforms to facilitate communication and coordination among team members.

Moreover, ensuring the security and privacy of software applications presents a significant challenge for developers. With the increasing frequency and sophistication of cyber attacks, developers must prioritize security throughout the software development lifecycle. This includes implementing secure coding practices, conducting regular security assessments, and staying informed about emerging threats and vulnerabilities. Additionally, developers must comply with data protection regulations such as GDPR and HIPAA, which impose strict requirements for handling sensitive data. To address these challenges, developers can incorporate security into their development process from the outset and employ tools such as static code analysis, penetration testing, and encryption to mitigate security risks.

Furthermore, maintaining software quality while meeting tight deadlines is a perennial challenge for development teams. With the pressure to deliver features quickly, developers may prioritize speed over quality, leading to technical debt, bugs, and usability issues. To strike a balance between speed and quality, developers can adopt agile development methodologies such as Scrum or Kanban, which emphasize iterative development and continuous feedback. Additionally, automated testing tools and continuous integration/continuous deployment (CI/CD) pipelines can help identify and address defects early in the development process, reducing the likelihood of costly rework later on.

In summary, modern software development presents a myriad of challenges for developers, ranging from technological complexity and collaboration issues to security concerns and time constraints. By identifying and understanding these challenges, developers can devise effective strategies to overcome them and deliver successful software projects. Embracing best practices, staying abreast of emerging technologies, and fostering a culture of collaboration and continuous improvement are essential for addressing the challenges of modern software development and achieving success in today's competitive marketplace.

Addressing complexity in development projects is paramount for ensuring successful outcomes in software engineering endeavors. With the ever-evolving landscape of technology and the increasing demands for sophisticated solutions, developers encounter various challenges related to managing complexity throughout the development lifecycle.

One strategy for managing complexity is adopting a modular approach to software design. By breaking down large systems into smaller, more manageable modules or components, developers can isolate functionality, reduce dependencies, and improve maintainability. Command-line tools such as npm or pip can facilitate modular development by allowing developers to install and manage dependencies easily. For example, in a Node.js project, developers can use npm to install external libraries or frameworks, such as Express.js or React, which provide modular components for building web applications.

Furthermore, employing design patterns can help address complexity by providing reusable solutions to common design problems. Design patterns such as the Observer pattern, Factory pattern, or Singleton pattern can help streamline development, improve code readability, and promote consistency across projects. CLI commands such as git clone or npm install can facilitate the integration of design patterns into projects by allowing developers to clone repositories or install packages that implement these patterns. For instance, developers can use git clone to fetch a repository containing a template for implementing the Observer pattern in a Java project.

Another strategy for managing complexity is prioritizing simplicity in software architecture and implementation. Complex solutions often lead to increased cognitive load, making it challenging for developers to understand, maintain, and extend codebases over time. By favoring simplicity over complexity, developers can reduce the risk of introducing bugs and improve the overall maintainability of their code. Command-line tools such as git diff or git log can help developers review changes and track the evolution of codebases, enabling them to identify areas where simplification may be beneficial. For example, developers can use git diff to compare different versions of a file and identify areas of complexity or redundancy that could be refactored for improved clarity.

Moreover, embracing test-driven development (TDD) can help mitigate complexity by encouraging developers to write tests before writing code. TDD promotes a modular, incremental approach to development, where developers write small, focused tests that drive the implementation of features. By writing tests upfront, developers can gain a deeper understanding of requirements, identify edge cases early, and design more modular and maintainable code. Command-line tools such as Jest or pytest can facilitate test-driven development by providing frameworks for writing and running tests in various programming languages. For example, developers can use Jest to write unit tests for a JavaScript application and run them from the command line using the npm test command.

Furthermore, establishing clear communication channels and fostering collaboration among team members can help address complexity in development projects. By promoting transparency, sharing knowledge, and soliciting feedback, teams can leverage the collective expertise of their members to tackle complex problems more effectively. Collaboration tools such as Slack, Microsoft Teams, or Jira can facilitate communication and coordination among team members, enabling them to collaborate on tasks, share updates, and resolve issues in real-time. For example, teams can use Slack channels to discuss project requirements, share code snippets, and coordinate development efforts across distributed teams.

Additionally, prioritizing documentation and knowledge sharing can help mitigate complexity by ensuring that critical information is accessible to all team members. By documenting design decisions, APIs, and system architecture, developers can reduce the cognitive load associated with understanding complex systems and facilitate onboarding for new team members. Command-line tools such as Javadoc or Sphinx can assist in generating documentation from code comments or Markdown files, making it easier for developers to create and maintain documentation alongside their code. For instance, developers can use Javadoc to generate API documentation for a Java project and deploy it to a web server using the javadoc command.

In summary, addressing complexity in development projects requires a multifaceted approach that encompasses modular design, design patterns, simplicity, test-driven development, collaboration, and documentation. By employing these strategies, developers can effectively manage complexity, improve code quality, and deliver successful software projects that meet the needs of stakeholders. Embracing simplicity, fostering collaboration, and prioritizing documentation are essential for navigating the complexities of modern software development and achieving long-term success in an ever-changing landscape.

Chapter 2: Advanced Strategies for Harnessing Copilot

Advanced techniques for interacting with Copilot suggestions can significantly enhance productivity and code quality for developers. As Copilot continues to evolve, mastering these techniques becomes increasingly important for maximizing its potential in various development scenarios.

One advanced technique is leveraging Copilot's context-awareness to refine and customize suggestions based on specific coding tasks. By providing additional context through comments or surrounding code, developers can guide Copilot to generate more accurate and relevant suggestions. For example, when working on a particular function or method, developers can add comments or type declarations to provide Copilot with information about expected inputs and outputs, helping it generate more tailored code snippets. Additionally, developers can use the "--context" flag with the "copilot autocomplete" command to specify context directly from the command line, ensuring that Copilot considers the relevant context when making suggestions.

Another advanced technique is understanding and manipulating the underlying machine learning models used by Copilot to generate suggestions. While Copilot's models are proprietary and not directly accessible to developers, understanding the principles of machine learning and natural language processing can provide insights into how Copilot functions and how to optimize its performance. Developers can experiment with different coding styles, patterns, and inputs to observe how Copilot responds and iteratively improve its suggestions over time. Additionally, developers can explore research papers, blog posts, and documentation related to machine learning and programming language models to gain a deeper understanding of the techniques employed by Copilot.

Furthermore, developers can customize Copilot's behavior and preferences to better align with their individual coding style and preferences. Copilot offers various settings and configurations that developers can adjust to tailor its suggestions to their specific needs. For example, developers can enable or disable specific programming languages, libraries, or frameworks to narrow down the scope of suggestions to those relevant to their project. Additionally, developers can adjust the verbosity level of suggestions, the frequency of suggestions, and the types of code snippets generated by Copilot. By fine-tuning these settings, developers can optimize Copilot's performance and integrate it seamlessly into their development workflow.

Moreover, developers can collaborate with Copilot to co-create code in real-time, leveraging its suggestions as a virtual pair programmer. By actively engaging with Copilot during the coding process, developers can iterate on its suggestions, refine code snippets, and explore alternative solutions collaboratively. This interactive approach allows developers to leverage Copilot's expertise while retaining control and oversight over the codebase. Additionally, developers can use code review tools and version control systems such as GitHub to review and manage changes made by Copilot, ensuring code quality and consistency across the project.

Additionally, developers can combine Copilot's suggestions with other productivity tools and techniques to further enhance their coding experience. For example, developers can integrate Copilot with code linters, static analysis tools, and automated testing frameworks to enforce coding standards, identify potential issues, and ensure code quality. By incorporating Copilot into their existing development toolchain, developers can leverage its capabilities alongside other tools and techniques to streamline their workflow and produce high-quality code more efficiently.

Furthermore, developers can explore advanced strategies for interpreting and evaluating Copilot suggestions, taking into account factors such as code readability, performance, and maintainability. While Copilot excels at generating code snippets quickly, developers must exercise judgment and critical thinking when incorporating its suggestions into their projects. By considering the broader context of their codebase, project requirements, and coding standards, developers can make informed decisions about which suggestions to accept, modify, or reject. Additionally, developers can use code review processes and peer feedback to validate Copilot suggestions and ensure that they align with project goals and best practices.

In summary, mastering advanced techniques for interacting with Copilot suggestions is essential for developers seeking to harness its full potential in their development workflow. By leveraging context-awareness, understanding machine learning models, customizing preferences, collaborating interactively, integrating with other tools, and exercising judgment, developers can optimize Copilot's performance and produce high-quality code more efficiently. As Copilot continues to evolve, developers must stay abreast of new features, techniques, and best practices to unlock its full capabilities and drive innovation in software development.

Harnessing Copilot for complex problem-solving scenarios requires a deep understanding of its capabilities and effective utilization of advanced techniques. Copilot, powered by state-of-the-art artificial intelligence models, can assist developers in tackling a wide range of intricate problems across various domains. By leveraging Copilot's vast knowledge base and contextual understanding, developers can expedite the process of problem-solving and produce high-quality solutions efficiently.

One key aspect of harnessing Copilot for complex problem-solving is providing clear and precise input to guide its suggestions effectively. Developers can use specific comments, type annotations, or contextual information within the code to convey the problem statement, constraints, and desired outcomes to Copilot. By framing the problem in a structured manner, developers can enhance Copilot's understanding and increase the likelihood of generating relevant and accurate suggestions. Additionally, developers can utilize the "copilot autocomplete" command with the "--context" flag to provide explicit context from the command line, ensuring that Copilot considers the relevant information when generating suggestions.

Furthermore, developers can explore Copilot's ability to synthesize code snippets from natural language descriptions of problems or tasks. By articulating the problem in plain English or other supported languages, developers can prompt Copilot to generate code based on the provided description. This approach is particularly useful for brainstorming ideas, exploring alternative solutions, and quickly prototyping implementations for complex problems. Developers can experiment with different variations of problem descriptions and iterate on Copilot's suggestions to refine their understanding of the problem space and identify optimal solutions.

Moreover, developers can leverage Copilot's collaborative capabilities to engage in interactive problem-solving sessions. By actively collaborating with Copilot, developers can co-create code in real-time, refining suggestions, exploring alternative approaches, and iteratively solving complex problems. This interactive approach allows developers to leverage Copilot's expertise while retaining control and oversight over the problem-solving process. Additionally, developers can use version control systems such as Git to track changes, review iterations, and manage contributions made by Copilot, ensuring transparency and accountability in the problem-solving workflow.

Additionally, developers can integrate Copilot with domain-specific libraries, frameworks, and tools to address complex problems effectively. By leveraging existing libraries and frameworks tailored to specific problem domains, developers can augment Copilot's capabilities and streamline the problem-solving process. For example, in the field of data science, developers can integrate Copilot with popular libraries such as NumPy, pandas, and scikit-learn to accelerate tasks such as data manipulation, analysis, and machine learning model development. By combining Copilot's code generation capabilities with domain-specific tools and techniques, developers can tackle complex problems more comprehensively and efficiently.

Furthermore, developers can harness Copilot's suggestions to implement algorithms, data structures, and optimization techniques for solving complex computational problems. Copilot's ability to synthesize code based on natural language descriptions allows developers to explore a wide range of algorithms and strategies for addressing diverse problem scenarios. By articulating problem requirements and algorithmic concepts in plain language, developers can prompt Copilot to generate code implementations, visualize data structures, and prototype algorithms iteratively. Additionally, developers can use Copilot to explore performance optimizations, algorithmic trade-offs, and scalability considerations for complex problem-solving tasks.

Moreover, developers can leverage Copilot's integration with code review processes to validate solutions and ensure code quality for complex problem-solving scenarios. By soliciting feedback from peers, reviewing generated code snippets, and conducting thorough testing, developers can verify the correctness, efficiency, and robustness of their solutions. Additionally, developers can use code review tools and static analysis techniques to identify potential issues, refactor code, and enforce coding standards, enhancing the reliability and maintainability of solutions developed with Copilot.

In summary, harnessing Copilot for complex problem-solving scenarios requires a combination of effective input framing, interactive collaboration, integration with domain-specific tools, exploration of algorithmic techniques, and validation through code review processes. By leveraging Copilot's AI capabilities, developers can streamline the problem-solving process, explore innovative solutions, and accelerate development cycles for complex problem domains. As Copilot continues to evolve, developers must stay abreast of new features, techniques, and best practices to unlock its full potential and drive innovation in problem-solving.

Chapter 3: Deep Dive into Copilot's AI Models

Exploring Copilot's neural network architecture provides valuable insights into how the platform generates code suggestions and assists developers in various programming tasks. While the inner workings of Copilot's architecture are proprietary, understanding the general principles of neural network design can shed light on its functioning. Copilot is built on a deep learning architecture, likely employing recurrent neural networks (RNNs), transformers, or a combination of both to process natural language input and generate code outputs.

At its core, Copilot's neural network architecture consists of multiple layers of interconnected nodes, each responsible for different aspects of processing and generating code. The architecture is trained on vast amounts of code from public repositories, enabling it to learn patterns, idioms, and conventions commonly found in software development. The neural network architecture is designed to encode the semantics and syntax of programming languages, allowing Copilot to understand context, infer intent, and generate code that aligns with the developer's requirements.

One key component of Copilot's neural network architecture is its ability to handle natural language input effectively. Natural language processing (NLP) techniques are employed to preprocess and encode textual input, enabling Copilot to understand human-readable descriptions of programming tasks, requirements, and constraints. This involves tokenization, embedding, and semantic analysis of text data, allowing Copilot to extract relevant information and generate code suggestions based on the input provided.

Additionally, Copilot's neural network architecture likely incorporates attention mechanisms to focus on relevant parts of the input and output sequences during processing. Attention mechanisms enable Copilot to weigh the importance of different words or tokens in the input text, allowing it to attend to key information and generate contextually appropriate code suggestions. This attention mechanism enhances Copilot's ability to understand complex sentences, handle ambiguity, and produce coherent code outputs.

Furthermore, Copilot's neural network architecture may include recurrent layers or transformer layers to model sequential dependencies and long-range dependencies in the input text. Recurrent layers, such as long short-term memory (LSTM) or gated recurrent units (GRUs), enable Copilot to capture temporal dependencies and contextual information across multiple tokens in the input text. This is particularly important for understanding the flow of code, handling nested structures, and generating syntactically correct code snippets.

Moreover, transformer-based architectures, such as the popular BERT (Bidirectional Encoder Representations from Transformers) model, may be utilized to process natural language input and generate code suggestions.

Transformers excel at capturing global dependencies and contextual information in text data, making them well-suited for tasks such as code completion, code summarization, and code generation. Copilot's transformer-based architecture likely leverages pre-trained language models fine-tuned on code-related tasks to enhance its performance and effectiveness.

Additionally, Copilot's neural network architecture may incorporate reinforcement learning techniques to improve its performance over time through interaction with developers and feedback from code reviews. Reinforcement learning enables Copilot to learn from its experiences, refine its predictions, and adapt to the preferences and coding style of individual developers. By rewarding desirable behaviors and penalizing undesirable behaviors, Copilot's neural network architecture can iteratively improve its code generation capabilities and provide more accurate and relevant suggestions.

In summary, exploring Copilot's neural network architecture provides valuable insights into how the platform operates and assists developers in their coding tasks. While the specific details of Copilot's architecture are proprietary, understanding general principles of neural network design, such as natural language processing, attention mechanisms, recurrent layers, transformers, and reinforcement learning, can help developers appreciate the sophistication and capabilities of Copilot's underlying technology. As Copilot continues to evolve and incorporate advances in AI and machine learning, developers can expect further enhancements in its code generation capabilities and support for a wider range of programming tasks.

Understanding Copilot's learning and adaptation mechanisms is essential for developers seeking to leverage its capabilities effectively in their coding endeavors. Copilot employs a sophisticated blend of machine learning techniques to continuously improve its performance and adapt to the specific needs and preferences of individual users. At the heart of Copilot's learning and adaptation mechanisms lies its ability to analyze vast amounts of code data, learn from user interactions, and refine its code generation capabilities over time.

One of the key learning mechanisms employed by Copilot is supervised learning, which involves training the model on labeled datasets of code examples. During the training process, Copilot's neural network architecture analyzes pairs of input-output code snippets, learning to map natural language descriptions to corresponding code implementations. This supervised learning approach enables Copilot to understand the relationships between textual descriptions of programming tasks and the corresponding code solutions, allowing it to generate accurate and contextually relevant code suggestions.

Additionally, Copilot leverages unsupervised learning techniques to uncover patterns, structures, and regularities in unannotated code data. Unsupervised learning algorithms, such as clustering and dimensionality reduction, enable Copilot to identify common coding idioms, recognize recurring patterns, and extract useful features from code repositories. By analyzing large volumes of code without explicit labels, Copilot can discover implicit knowledge and generalize its understanding of programming concepts across different domains and languages.

Furthermore, Copilot employs reinforcement learning (RL) to improve its performance through interaction with users and feedback from code reviews. RL algorithms enable Copilot to learn from its actions, receiving rewards or penalties based on the quality and relevance of its code suggestions. By iteratively adjusting its behavior in response to feedback, Copilot can learn to prioritize certain coding patterns, avoid common mistakes, and adapt to the coding style and preferences of individual users. This adaptive learning process allows Copilot to continually refine its code generation capabilities and provide more personalized and effective assistance to developers.

Moreover, Copilot incorporates active learning techniques to intelligently select and prioritize training examples for further annotation or feedback. Active learning algorithms analyze user interactions, identifying instances where Copilot's predictions are uncertain or ambiguous. By requesting additional input or clarification from users in these uncertain cases, Copilot can improve its understanding of complex programming tasks and expand its knowledge base over time. This iterative process of active learning allows Copilot to focus its training efforts on the most informative and challenging examples, accelerating its learning and adaptation process.

Additionally, Copilot employs transfer learning to leverage pre-existing knowledge and models trained on large-scale datasets of code. Transfer learning enables Copilot to benefit from the knowledge acquired during pre-training on general code-related tasks, such as code completion, code summarization, and code translation. By fine-tuning pre-trained models on domain-specific datasets or user interactions, Copilot can quickly adapt to new programming languages, frameworks, or project requirements, without requiring extensive retraining from scratch.

Furthermore, Copilot incorporates contextual learning mechanisms to capture the context and intent of programming tasks beyond individual code snippets. Contextual learning involves analyzing the surrounding code, comments, and documentation to infer the developer's intentions and preferences. By considering the broader context of a coding project or task, Copilot can generate more accurate and contextually relevant code suggestions, taking into account factors such as variable names, function calls, and code patterns.

In summary, understanding Copilot's learning and adaptation mechanisms is crucial for developers looking to harness its full potential in their coding workflows. By leveraging a combination of supervised learning, unsupervised learning, reinforcement learning, active learning, transfer learning, and contextual learning techniques, Copilot continuously refines its code generation capabilities, adapts to user preferences, and provides personalized assistance tailored to individual coding tasks. As Copilot evolves and incorporates advancements in artificial intelligence and machine learning, developers can expect further improvements in its learning and adaptation capabilities, enhancing its effectiveness as a productivity tool for software development.

Chapter 4: Navigating Legal and Ethical Considerations

Legal implications of using AI in software development are a crucial consideration for developers and organizations navigating the rapidly evolving landscape of artificial intelligence (AI) technology. As AI systems, including tools like GitHub Copilot, become increasingly integrated into software development workflows, they raise complex legal questions and potential risks related to intellectual property rights, data privacy, liability, and regulatory compliance.

One of the primary legal concerns surrounding the use of AI in software development is the ownership and protection of intellectual property (IP) rights. When developers use AI tools like Copilot to generate code, questions arise regarding the ownership of the resulting code snippets and whether they qualify for copyright protection. While copyright laws typically grant protection to original works of authorship, including software code, the involvement of AI algorithms in the code generation process complicates matters. Developers must consider whether AI-generated code constitutes a derivative work, a joint work, or a work of the AI itself, impacting the ownership and licensing of the code and potentially leading to disputes over ownership rights.

Moreover, the use of AI in software development raises concerns about potential infringement of third-party intellectual property rights. Developers must ensure that AI-generated code does not violate existing patents, copyrights, or trademarks owned by others. AI tools like Copilot, while designed to assist developers in generating original code, may inadvertently produce code that infringes upon existing intellectual property rights. Therefore, developers should conduct thorough due diligence, including patent searches and code reviews, to identify and mitigate any potential infringement risks before integrating AI-generated code into their projects.

Another legal consideration related to AI in software development is data privacy and security. AI algorithms, including those powering tools like Copilot, often require access to large datasets of code in order to learn and generate accurate code suggestions. However, the use of such datasets may raise privacy concerns, particularly if they contain sensitive or proprietary information. Developers must ensure compliance with relevant data protection laws, such as the General Data Protection Regulation (GDPR) in Europe or the California Consumer Privacy Act (CCPA) in the United States, by obtaining appropriate consent, anonymizing data, or implementing data protection measures to safeguard user privacy and confidentiality.

Furthermore, the deployment of AI in software development introduces potential liability risks for developers and organizations. If AI-generated code produces errors, vulnerabilities, or unintended consequences that result in financial losses, property damage, or personal injury, the parties involved may be held liable for negligence or product liability.

Developers should carefully assess and mitigate the risks associated with using AI tools in their software development processes, including implementing rigorous testing, quality assurance measures, and error handling mechanisms to minimize the likelihood of adverse outcomes.

Additionally, the regulatory landscape surrounding AI technology is evolving rapidly, with lawmakers and regulatory agencies seeking to address the legal and ethical challenges posed by AI in various domains, including software development. Developers must stay informed about relevant laws, regulations, and guidelines governing the use of AI in their jurisdiction, as well as emerging best practices and industry standards for ethical AI development and deployment. Compliance with regulatory requirements, such as transparency, fairness, accountability, and non-discrimination, is essential to mitigate legal risks and build trust in AI-powered software solutions.

In summary, the legal implications of using AI in software development are multifaceted and require careful consideration by developers, organizations, and policymakers alike. From intellectual property rights and data privacy to liability and regulatory compliance, the legal landscape surrounding AI technology is complex and dynamic. Developers must navigate these legal challenges responsibly, taking proactive measures to address potential risks and ensure compliance with applicable laws and regulations, while also fostering innovation and advancing the responsible use of AI in software development.

Ethical guidelines for responsible AI implementation are essential in guiding the development, deployment, and use of artificial intelligence (AI) systems in a manner that upholds ethical principles, respects human rights, and promotes societal well-being. As AI technologies continue to advance and permeate various aspects of society, including healthcare, finance, transportation, and more, it is imperative to establish ethical frameworks to ensure that AI applications are developed and deployed ethically and responsibly.

One of the fundamental principles underlying ethical AI implementation is fairness. AI systems should be designed and trained to treat all individuals fairly and without bias, regardless of their race, gender, ethnicity, religion, or other characteristics. To achieve fairness, developers must carefully select and preprocess training data to minimize biases and ensure equitable outcomes. Additionally, algorithms should be regularly monitored and audited to detect and mitigate any biases that may arise during the development or deployment phases.

Transparency is another key principle in ethical AI implementation. Developers should strive to make AI systems transparent and understandable to end-users, stakeholders, and regulatory authorities. This includes providing clear explanations of how AI algorithms work, what data they use, and how they make decisions. Transparency promotes accountability and trust, enabling users to understand and challenge AI decisions and facilitating regulatory oversight and compliance. Accountability is closely linked to transparency and involves holding individuals and organizations responsible for the design, development, and deployment of AI systems. Developers should establish clear lines of accountability and mechanisms for recourse in cases where AI systems cause harm or fail to meet ethical standards. This may include implementing codes of conduct, establishing ethical review boards, and providing channels for feedback and redress.

Privacy and data protection are paramount considerations in ethical AI implementation, particularly as AI systems often require access to vast amounts of data to learn and make predictions. Developers must ensure that AI applications comply with relevant data protection laws and regulations, such as the General Data Protection Regulation (GDPR) in Europe or the Health Insurance Portability and Accountability Act (HIPAA) in the United States. This includes obtaining informed consent from individuals whose data is used, anonymizing data to protect privacy, and implementing robust security measures to prevent unauthorized access or data breaches.

Moreover, ethical AI implementation should prioritize safety and security to mitigate potential risks and harm to individuals and society. Developers must conduct thorough risk assessments and safety tests to identify and address potential hazards associated with AI systems, such as algorithmic errors, biases, or unintended consequences. Additionally, cybersecurity measures should be implemented to safeguard AI systems against malicious attacks or exploitation.

Ensuring inclusivity and accessibility is another ethical imperative in AI implementation. Developers should strive to design AI systems that are accessible to all individuals, including those with disabilities or marginalized communities. This may involve considering diverse user needs and preferences, providing alternative interfaces or modalities, and incorporating feedback from diverse stakeholders throughout the development process.

Finally, ethical AI implementation requires ongoing monitoring, evaluation, and adaptation to address emerging ethical challenges and societal concerns. Developers should establish mechanisms for continuous ethical review and reflection, including ethical impact assessments, stakeholder engagement, and interdisciplinary collaboration with experts in ethics, law, sociology, and other relevant fields.

In summary, ethical guidelines for responsible AI implementation are essential to ensure that AI technologies are developed and deployed in a manner that respects human rights, promotes fairness and transparency, protects privacy and data security, prioritizes safety and inclusivity, and upholds societal values and norms. By adhering to ethical principles and best practices, developers can harness the potential of AI to benefit individuals and society while minimizing risks and unintended consequences.

Chapter 5: Integrating Copilot with Legacy Systems

Integrating GitHub Copilot with legacy codebases presents several challenges due to differences in coding styles, conventions, and technologies between the existing code and Copilot's suggestions. One of the primary challenges is ensuring compatibility between Copilot-generated code and the existing codebase, particularly when dealing with older programming languages or outdated frameworks that may not be fully supported by Copilot's AI models. To address this challenge, developers can employ several strategies to facilitate the integration process and maximize the benefits of using Copilot with legacy codebases.

One strategy is to start small and focus on specific modules or components within the legacy codebase that can benefit from Copilot's assistance. By identifying isolated areas where Copilot's suggestions can be easily integrated and tested, developers can gradually expand the scope of integration while minimizing the risk of introducing errors or conflicts with existing code. This incremental approach allows developers to gain confidence in Copilot's capabilities and assess its impact on the overall codebase.

Another challenge in integrating Copilot with legacy codebases is maintaining consistency and coherence in coding style and architecture. Legacy codebases often lack uniformity in coding conventions and may exhibit spaghetti code or outdated design patterns that can hinder the effectiveness of Copilot's suggestions. To overcome this challenge, developers can establish coding guidelines and standards that align with Copilot's recommendations, ensuring a cohesive and maintainable codebase.

Furthermore, developers can leverage Copilot's ability to understand natural language descriptions and translate them into code to document and refactor legacy codebases. By providing descriptive comments or explanations alongside Copilot-generated code, developers can improve code readability and comprehension, making it easier to understand and maintain legacy systems over time.

One of the key challenges in integrating Copilot with legacy codebases is ensuring the security and stability of the resulting code. Legacy systems may contain vulnerabilities or dependencies that could be inadvertently exposed or compromised by integrating Copilot-generated code. To mitigate this risk, developers should thoroughly review and test Copilot suggestions before incorporating them into production code, using automated testing tools and security scanners to identify and address potential vulnerabilities.

Moreover, developers can use Copilot to automate repetitive or tedious tasks in legacy codebases, such as refactoring, code cleanup, or dependency management. By leveraging Copilot's ability to generate code snippets and refactorings based on natural language descriptions, developers can streamline the maintenance and modernization of legacy systems, reducing manual effort and minimizing the risk of human error.

Another challenge in integrating Copilot with legacy codebases is ensuring compliance with regulatory requirements and industry standards. Legacy systems may be subject to specific regulations or standards that govern data privacy, security, or performance, requiring careful consideration and validation of Copilot-generated code to ensure compliance. To address this challenge, developers can use Copilot to augment existing compliance processes and controls, incorporating automated checks and validations to ensure that Copilot-generated code meets regulatory requirements.

In summary, integrating Copilot with legacy codebases presents several challenges related to compatibility, consistency, security, and compliance. However, by employing strategies such as starting small, establishing coding standards, documenting code changes, testing rigorously, automating tasks, and ensuring compliance, developers can overcome these challenges and leverage Copilot to enhance the maintainability, efficiency, and security of legacy systems.

Refactoring legacy systems with the assistance of GitHub Copilot presents a multifaceted endeavor aimed at modernizing outdated codebases while preserving functionality, improving maintainability, and enhancing overall system performance. The process of refactoring legacy systems involves restructuring existing code to align with modern coding standards, design patterns, and best practices, all while minimizing disruptions to existing functionality and mitigating the risk of introducing bugs or regressions.

One of the primary challenges in refactoring legacy systems is identifying areas of the codebase that can benefit from refactoring while balancing the need to maintain backward compatibility and minimize the risk of introducing new issues. GitHub Copilot can play a crucial role in this process by analyzing the existing codebase and providing intelligent suggestions for refactoring opportunities based on established coding conventions, design patterns, and code quality metrics. Developers can leverage Copilot's AI-powered assistance to identify areas of code that are candidates for refactoring, such as duplicated code, overly complex algorithms, or outdated libraries and dependencies.

Once potential refactoring opportunities have been identified, developers can use Copilot to generate refactoring suggestions tailored to the specific context of the codebase. For example, Copilot can provide automated refactorings for extracting methods, renaming variables, consolidating duplicate code, or introducing more efficient data structures and algorithms. By following Copilot's suggestions, developers can expedite the refactoring process and ensure consistency and correctness in the resulting code.

Furthermore, Copilot can assist developers in adopting modern coding practices and design patterns during the refactoring process. For instance, Copilot can suggest the use of object-oriented principles such as encapsulation, inheritance, and polymorphism to improve the structure and organization of the codebase. Additionally, Copilot can recommend the adoption of design patterns such as the Singleton pattern, Factory pattern, or Observer pattern to address common design challenges and improve code maintainability and extensibility. Another aspect of refactoring legacy systems with Copilot assistance is ensuring that the refactored codebase remains compatible with the existing system architecture and external dependencies. Copilot can help developers navigate these complexities by providing context-aware suggestions that take into account the existing codebase's structure, dependencies, and integration points. Additionally, developers can use Copilot to generate unit tests and integration tests to validate the correctness of the refactored code and ensure that it behaves as expected within the larger system.

In addition to code-level refactorings, Copilot can also assist in refactoring documentation, comments, and other non-code artifacts within the legacy codebase. For example, Copilot can suggest improvements to code comments, Javadoc annotations, or README files to ensure that they accurately reflect the changes introduced during the refactoring process. By maintaining clear and up-to-date documentation, developers can facilitate collaboration and knowledge sharing within the development team and across the organization.

Moreover, Copilot can help developers refactor legacy systems to address performance bottlenecks, scalability issues, and security vulnerabilities. For example, Copilot can suggest optimizations such as algorithmic improvements, caching strategies, or database schema optimizations to improve system performance and scalability. Additionally, Copilot can identify potential security vulnerabilities such as SQL injection, cross-site scripting, or authentication bypasses and provide suggestions for mitigating these risks through code refactoring and security best practices.

Furthermore, Copilot can assist in refactoring legacy systems to adopt modern software development methodologies and tools such as continuous integration, continuous deployment, and DevOps practices. By integrating Copilot into the development workflow, developers can automate repetitive tasks, streamline code reviews, and accelerate the delivery of high-quality software updates to production. Additionally, Copilot can provide guidance on incorporating test-driven development, code reviews, and peer feedback into the refactoring process to ensure code quality and maintainability.

In summary, refactoring legacy systems with Copilot assistance is a complex yet rewarding endeavor that requires careful planning, collaboration, and attention to detail. By leveraging Copilot's AI-powered assistance, developers can identify refactoring opportunities, adopt modern coding practices and design patterns, ensure compatibility and correctness, and improve system performance and security. Through iterative refactoring and continuous improvement, developers can modernize legacy systems and unlock new opportunities for innovation and growth.

Chapter 6: Handling Security Concerns with Copilot

Security best practices for using Copilot in development are crucial to ensure the integrity, confidentiality, and availability of sensitive code and data. With the growing adoption of AI-powered tools like Copilot in software development workflows, it's essential for developers and organizations to understand and implement robust security measures to mitigate potential risks and vulnerabilities.

One of the primary security considerations when using Copilot is data privacy and confidentiality. Since Copilot operates by analyzing code snippets and providing contextually relevant suggestions, developers must be cautious not to expose sensitive or proprietary information in the code they share with the tool. This includes avoiding the inclusion of hardcoded credentials, API keys, or other sensitive data in code samples that are used with Copilot. Instead, developers should utilize secure credential management practices, such as storing sensitive information in environment variables or secure configuration files, and avoid committing such data to version control repositories.

Additionally, developers should be mindful of the security implications of sharing proprietary or confidential code with Copilot, particularly in cases where the code contains intellectual property or trade secrets. Organizations should establish clear policies and guidelines regarding the types of code that can be shared with Copilot and ensure that developers adhere to these policies to prevent inadvertent disclosure of sensitive information. Furthermore, organizations may consider implementing access controls and auditing mechanisms to monitor and track the usage of Copilot within their development environments.

Another security consideration when using Copilot is the potential for introducing security vulnerabilities or weaknesses into the codebase through the use of generated code suggestions. While Copilot aims to provide contextually relevant and syntactically correct code suggestions, there is always a risk of generating code that contains security flaws or vulnerabilities, such as SQL injection, cross-site scripting (XSS), or improper input validation. To mitigate this risk, developers should carefully review and validate the code suggestions provided by Copilot before integrating them into their codebase. This may involve conducting code reviews, performing security testing, and leveraging automated static analysis tools to identify and remediate potential security issues.

Furthermore, developers should be aware of the security implications of third-party dependencies and libraries that are recommended by Copilot. While third-party libraries can help accelerate development and reduce code complexity, they also introduce potential security risks, such as outdated or vulnerable dependencies, license compliance issues, or malicious code injection. To mitigate these risks, developers should carefully evaluate the trustworthiness and security posture of third-party libraries recommended by Copilot, prioritize the use of well-maintained and actively supported dependencies, and regularly update and patch dependencies to address known security vulnerabilities.

Additionally, organizations should consider implementing secure coding practices and standards when using Copilot to develop software applications. This includes following industry best practices for secure coding, such as input validation, output encoding, proper error handling, and secure authentication and authorization mechanisms. By adhering to secure coding practices, developers can reduce the likelihood of introducing security vulnerabilities into their codebase and minimize the risk of exploitation by malicious actors.

Moreover, organizations should implement robust security controls and monitoring mechanisms to detect and respond to security incidents or anomalies related to the use of Copilot. This may include implementing intrusion detection and prevention systems, log monitoring and analysis, security information and event management (SIEM) solutions, and threat intelligence feeds to identify and mitigate potential security threats or attacks targeting the development environment.

Furthermore, organizations should prioritize security awareness and training for developers who use Copilot to ensure that they are knowledgeable about common security risks and vulnerabilities and understand how to mitigate them effectively. This may involve providing developers with security training and education programs, conducting regular security awareness sessions, and promoting a culture of security within the organization.

In summary, security best practices for using Copilot in development are essential to mitigate potential risks and vulnerabilities associated with the use of AI-powered tools in software development workflows. By implementing robust security measures, organizations can protect sensitive code and data, mitigate the risk of introducing security vulnerabilities, and ensure the integrity and security of their software applications.

Mitigating security risks associated with Copilot integration is paramount for ensuring the safety and integrity of software development processes. As Copilot becomes an integral part of development workflows, it's crucial to implement robust security measures to safeguard against potential threats and vulnerabilities.

One of the primary security concerns when integrating Copilot is the protection of sensitive data and intellectual property. Since Copilot operates by analyzing code snippets and providing contextually relevant suggestions, there is a risk of inadvertently exposing proprietary information or sensitive data in the code shared with the tool. To mitigate this risk, developers must exercise caution when sharing code with Copilot and avoid including confidential information such as API keys, passwords, or proprietary algorithms in code samples.

A key aspect of mitigating security risks with Copilot integration is ensuring the confidentiality and integrity of code repositories. Developers should follow best practices for securing version control systems such as Git, including implementing access controls, encryption, and authentication mechanisms to restrict unauthorized access to code repositories. Additionally, organizations should regularly audit and monitor code repositories for any unauthorized changes or suspicious activity, and promptly address any security incidents or breaches.

Another important consideration for mitigating security risks with Copilot integration is the validation and review of code suggestions provided by the tool. While Copilot aims to provide helpful and contextually relevant code suggestions, there is a possibility of generating code that contains security vulnerabilities or weaknesses. Developers should carefully review and validate code suggestions from Copilot before integrating them into their codebase, and conduct thorough security testing to identify and remediate any potential vulnerabilities.

Furthermore, organizations should implement secure coding practices and standards when using Copilot to develop software applications. This includes following industry best practices for secure coding, such as input validation, output encoding, proper error handling, and secure authentication and authorization mechanisms. By adhering to secure coding practices, developers can reduce the likelihood of introducing security vulnerabilities into their codebase and minimize the risk of exploitation by malicious actors.

Additionally, organizations should consider the security implications of third-party dependencies and libraries recommended by Copilot. While third-party libraries can expedite development and reduce code complexity, they also introduce potential security risks such as outdated or vulnerable dependencies, license compliance issues, or malicious code injection. To mitigate these risks, developers should carefully evaluate the security posture of third-party dependencies recommended by Copilot, prioritize the use of well-maintained and actively supported libraries, and regularly update and patch dependencies to address known security vulnerabilities.

Moreover, organizations should implement robust security controls and monitoring mechanisms to detect and respond to security incidents or anomalies related to Copilot integration. This may include implementing intrusion detection and prevention systems, log monitoring and analysis, security information and event management (SIEM) solutions, and threat intelligence feeds to identify and mitigate potential security threats or attacks targeting the development environment.

Furthermore, security awareness and training for developers are essential for mitigating security risks associated with Copilot integration. Organizations should provide developers with security training and education programs to raise awareness about common security risks and vulnerabilities and ensure that developers understand how to mitigate them effectively. By promoting a culture of security within the organization and empowering developers with the knowledge and skills to address security challenges, organizations can enhance the overall security posture of their development workflows.

In summary, mitigating security risks associated with Copilot integration requires a comprehensive approach that includes protecting sensitive data, validating code suggestions, following secure coding practices, evaluating third-party dependencies, implementing robust security controls and monitoring mechanisms, and providing security awareness and training for developers. By implementing these measures, organizations can enhance the security of their development processes and minimize the risk of security breaches and vulnerabilities associated with Copilot integration.

Chapter 7: Extending Copilot's Capabilities through Customization

Customizing Copilot's suggestions and behaviors is essential for tailoring the tool to specific development workflows and preferences, allowing developers to optimize their productivity and efficiency. Copilot offers various customization options that enable users to personalize the tool's behavior, adjust its suggestions, and enhance its integration with existing development processes.

One of the key customization features of Copilot is the ability to adjust the sensitivity of its suggestions. By default, Copilot provides a wide range of suggestions based on the context of the code being written. However, users can customize the sensitivity level to fine-tune the frequency and relevance of suggestions according to their preferences. This can be achieved using the "--sensitivity" flag followed by a sensitivity level parameter when invoking Copilot from the command line interface (CLI), allowing users to specify whether they prefer more conservative or aggressive suggestions.

Additionally, developers can customize Copilot's suggestions by providing feedback on the relevance and quality of the generated code snippets. This feedback loop helps improve Copilot's machine learning models over time and ensures that the tool delivers more accurate and contextually relevant suggestions in future interactions. Users can provide feedback directly within the integrated development environment (IDE) by rating the usefulness of individual suggestions or flagging irrelevant or incorrect code snippets.

Furthermore, Copilot offers customization options for incorporating coding conventions and style preferences into its suggestions. Developers can specify their preferred coding style, formatting rules, and naming conventions using configuration files or settings within their IDE. By aligning Copilot's suggestions with the established coding standards of the project or organization, developers can maintain consistency and coherence across the codebase while leveraging the tool's assistance.

Another aspect of customizing Copilot's behavior is integrating it with code linting and static analysis tools to enforce coding standards and best practices automatically. By incorporating Copilot's suggestions into existing linting pipelines, developers can ensure that the generated code complies with predefined rules and guidelines, such as identifying potential bugs, enforcing coding conventions, and optimizing performance. This integration helps streamline the development process and reduces the need for manual code reviews and corrections.

Moreover, developers can customize Copilot's behavior by creating custom code templates and shortcuts tailored to specific use cases or programming languages. This allows developers to quickly generate boilerplate code, common patterns, or frequently used snippets with minimal effort. Custom templates can be defined using simple text files or code generation tools and integrated into Copilot's suggestion engine, enabling users to access them easily while coding.

Additionally, Copilot offers integration with version control systems such as Git, allowing developers to leverage historical code repositories and project-specific contexts to enhance the relevance and accuracy of its suggestions. By analyzing the code history and context of the project, Copilot can provide more contextually relevant suggestions and anticipate the developer's intent more accurately. This integration can be enabled by configuring Copilot to access the repository and project metadata using Git commands or IDE plugins.

Furthermore, Copilot's suggestions and behaviors can be customized based on the specific requirements and constraints of different programming tasks or domains. For example, developers working on security-sensitive projects may prefer to disable suggestions that involve external dependencies or third-party libraries to minimize the risk of introducing vulnerabilities. Similarly, developers working on performance-critical applications may adjust Copilot's suggestions to prioritize code optimizations and efficiency improvements.

In summary, customizing Copilot's suggestions and behaviors allows developers to tailor the tool to their specific needs and preferences, enabling them to optimize their productivity, maintain coding standards, and streamline the development process. By adjusting the sensitivity of suggestions, providing feedback on the relevance and quality of code snippets, incorporating coding conventions and style preferences, integrating with linting and static analysis tools, creating custom code templates and shortcuts, leveraging version control system integration, and adapting to the requirements of different programming tasks or domains, developers can harness the full potential of Copilot to enhance their coding experience and deliver high-quality software more efficiently.

Building custom plugins and extensions for Copilot expands its functionality and allows developers to tailor the tool to specific workflows and requirements, empowering them to enhance their productivity and streamline their development process further. Custom plugins and extensions enable users to extend Copilot's capabilities beyond its out-of-the-box features, integrating it seamlessly with other tools, automating repetitive tasks, and providing domain-specific functionality.

One of the primary benefits of building custom plugins and extensions for Copilot is the ability to integrate it with existing development tools and platforms. By creating plugins that interface with popular IDEs, text editors, or integrated development environments, developers can access Copilot's suggestions directly within their preferred coding environment, eliminating the need to switch between multiple applications. This integration enhances the developer experience and enables a more seamless workflow by providing real-time access to Copilot's code generation capabilities while coding.

Furthermore, custom plugins and extensions can automate repetitive tasks and streamline common workflows by extending Copilot's functionality with additional features and automation capabilities. For example, developers can create plugins that automate code refactoring, generate documentation templates, perform static code analysis, or enforce coding standards and best practices. By automating these tasks, developers can save time and effort, reduce manual errors, and maintain consistency across their codebase more effectively.

Moreover, building custom plugins and extensions for Copilot allows developers to add domain-specific functionality and tailor the tool to the specific requirements of their projects or organizations. For instance, developers working in specialized domains such as machine learning, data science, or game development can create plugins that provide contextually relevant suggestions and code snippets specific to their field. These domain-specific plugins can accelerate development, facilitate knowledge sharing, and improve code quality by providing relevant guidance and assistance tailored to the specific domain.

In addition to enhancing Copilot's core functionality, custom plugins and extensions can extend its capabilities beyond code generation to support a wide range of development tasks and workflows. For example, developers can create plugins that integrate Copilot with project management tools, version control systems, continuous integration/continuous deployment (CI/CD) pipelines, or issue tracking systems.

These plugins enable developers to leverage Copilot's suggestions and insights across the entire software development lifecycle, from planning and coding to testing and deployment.

Furthermore, building custom plugins and extensions for Copilot fosters innovation and collaboration within the developer community by enabling users to share their plugins with others. By open-sourcing their plugins or contributing them to community-driven repositories, developers can leverage the collective expertise and creativity of the community to enhance Copilot's functionality and address common pain points. This collaborative approach promotes knowledge sharing, fosters community engagement, and accelerates the development of new features and capabilities for Copilot.

Additionally, building custom plugins and extensions for Copilot provides developers with an opportunity to experiment with new technologies, frameworks, and programming languages. By exploring the Copilot API and SDK, developers can gain insights into how machine learning models can be integrated into software development workflows and learn best practices for building intelligent developer tools. This hands-on experience with AI-powered code generation and assistance can broaden developers' skill sets and deepen their understanding of AI and machine learning concepts.

In summary, building custom plugins and extensions for Copilot offers developers a powerful way to extend its functionality, integrate it with existing tools and platforms, automate repetitive tasks, add domain-specific functionality, and foster innovation and collaboration within the developer community. By leveraging the Copilot API and SDK to create plugins that interface with popular IDEs, automate common workflows, support specialized domains, and enhance collaboration, developers can unlock new possibilities for enhancing their productivity and efficiency in software development.

Chapter 8: Building Scalable Solutions with Copilot

Leveraging Copilot for scalable software architectures presents a promising avenue for developers seeking to build robust, flexible, and maintainable systems capable of handling increasing complexity and user demands. Copilot, with its AI-driven code generation and assistance capabilities, offers valuable support in designing, implementing, and optimizing scalable architectures that can adapt and grow with evolving requirements and user needs.

One of the key ways developers can leverage Copilot for scalable software architectures is in the design phase, where they can use Copilot's suggestions to explore different architectural patterns, such as microservices, serverless, event-driven, or layered architectures. By analyzing Copilot's generated code snippets and suggestions, developers can gain insights into the pros and cons of each architectural approach and make informed decisions based on their project requirements, performance considerations, and scalability goals.

Once an architectural pattern is chosen, developers can use Copilot to scaffold the initial project structure and set up the foundational components, such as services, APIs, data models, and infrastructure configurations. By leveraging Copilot's code generation capabilities, developers can accelerate the development process and ensure consistency across the codebase, thereby reducing the risk of errors and simplifying maintenance tasks as the system evolves.

Furthermore, Copilot can assist developers in implementing scalability features, such as load balancing, horizontal scaling, caching, and asynchronous processing, which are essential for handling increasing workloads and user concurrency. By providing code snippets and best practices for implementing these features, Copilot enables developers to build scalable architectures that can efficiently distribute and manage resources to meet performance and availability requirements under varying conditions.

In addition to supporting the implementation of scalable architectures, Copilot can also help optimize existing systems for scalability by identifying performance bottlenecks, optimizing resource utilization, and refactoring code for improved scalability. By analyzing Copilot's suggestions and recommendations, developers can identify areas where optimization is needed, such as database queries, network calls, or computational-intensive tasks, and apply best practices and optimizations to improve system performance and scalability.

Moreover, Copilot can assist in automating deployment processes and infrastructure provisioning, which are crucial aspects of scaling software architectures. By generating deployment scripts, configuration files, and infrastructure as code templates, Copilot simplifies the deployment of scalable architectures across different environments, such as development, testing, staging, and production. This automation reduces the manual effort required for deploying and managing infrastructure, streamlines the release process, and ensures consistency and reliability across deployments.

Another way developers can leverage Copilot for scalable software architectures is in implementing fault tolerance and resilience mechanisms, such as retries, circuit breakers, and failover strategies. By providing code examples and guidance on implementing these patterns, Copilot helps developers build resilient systems capable of handling failures gracefully and maintaining availability and reliability under adverse conditions.

Furthermore, Copilot can assist in designing and implementing scalable data architectures, such as distributed databases, data lakes, and data warehouses, which are essential for managing large volumes of data and supporting analytics and reporting requirements. By providing code snippets and best practices for working with distributed data systems and data processing frameworks, Copilot enables developers to build scalable data architectures that can handle the growing demands of data-driven applications.

Additionally, Copilot can support the adoption of containerization and orchestration technologies, such as Docker and Kubernetes, which are foundational components of modern scalable architectures. By providing code snippets and templates for building containerized applications and deploying them to Kubernetes clusters, Copilot enables developers to leverage containerization and orchestration to achieve scalability, agility, and portability across different environments.

In summary, leveraging Copilot for scalable software architectures offers developers valuable support in designing, implementing, and optimizing systems that can scale gracefully to meet increasing demands and evolving requirements. By providing code generation, best practices, and automation capabilities, Copilot empowers developers to build scalable architectures that are robust, flexible, and maintainable, laying the foundation for successful and sustainable software projects.

Scaling Copilot usage for large-scale development projects involves leveraging its capabilities efficiently to address the challenges associated with managing complex codebases, collaborating with large teams, and ensuring consistent quality and productivity across the project. Copilot, with its AI-powered code suggestions and assistance, offers valuable support in scaling development efforts by accelerating coding tasks, promoting code consistency, and facilitating collaboration among team members.

One of the key strategies for scaling Copilot usage in large-scale development projects is to establish clear guidelines and best practices for incorporating Copilot into the development workflow. This includes defining coding standards, naming conventions, and project structures that align with the project's requirements and objectives. By providing developers with clear guidance on how to use Copilot effectively and efficiently, teams can ensure consistency and maintainability across the codebase, even as the project grows in size and complexity.

Moreover, integrating Copilot into the team's existing development tools and workflows is essential for scaling its usage effectively. This includes integrating Copilot with version control systems, such as Git, and development environments, such as Visual Studio Code or JetBrains IDEs, to streamline the process of accessing and incorporating Copilot's suggestions into the codebase. By integrating Copilot seamlessly into the development workflow, teams can maximize its impact on productivity and code quality while minimizing disruptions to the existing development process.

Another important aspect of scaling Copilot usage for large-scale projects is to empower developers with the necessary training and resources to make the most out of Copilot's capabilities. This includes providing training sessions, documentation, and tutorials on how to effectively use Copilot for various coding tasks, such as writing new code, refactoring existing code, or debugging issues. Additionally, fostering a culture of continuous learning and experimentation can encourage developers to explore new ways of leveraging Copilot to solve complex coding challenges and improve their productivity.

Furthermore, establishing effective communication channels and collaboration tools is crucial for scaling Copilot usage in large development teams. This includes using messaging platforms, such as Slack or Microsoft Teams, for real-time communication and collaboration, and project management tools, such as Jira or Asana, for tracking tasks and managing project progress. By fostering transparent communication and collaboration among team members, teams can ensure that everyone is aligned on project goals, priorities, and timelines, and can leverage Copilot's suggestions effectively to achieve them.

In addition to establishing clear guidelines and communication channels, it's important to monitor and measure the impact of Copilot usage on project productivity, code quality, and developer satisfaction. This includes tracking key metrics, such as code review feedback, code churn, and time to resolution, to assess the effectiveness of Copilot in improving development outcomes and identify areas for further optimization. By regularly reviewing and analyzing these metrics, teams can identify patterns and trends in Copilot usage and adjust their strategies accordingly to maximize its benefits.

Moreover, scaling Copilot usage for large-scale development projects requires ongoing maintenance and optimization to ensure its continued effectiveness and relevance. This includes regularly updating Copilot's training data and models to keep pace with evolving programming languages, frameworks, and best practices. Additionally, providing feedback to the Copilot team on areas where its suggestions can be improved or refined based on real-world usage can help drive continuous improvement and innovation in Copilot's capabilities.

In summary, scaling Copilot usage for large-scale development projects involves establishing clear guidelines, integrating Copilot into existing workflows, empowering developers with training and resources, fostering communication and collaboration, monitoring and measuring its impact, and optimizing its usage over time. By adopting these strategies, teams can leverage Copilot's capabilities effectively to accelerate development efforts, improve code quality, and drive innovation in large-scale software projects.

Chapter 9: Real-world Case Studies and Best Practices

Case studies of successful Copilot implementation in various industries offer valuable insights into how organizations leverage this AI-powered tool to streamline their software development processes, improve code quality, and enhance team collaboration. These real-world examples demonstrate the practical applications and benefits of integrating Copilot into different development workflows, highlighting its effectiveness in addressing common challenges and driving innovation in software development.

One notable case study is from a leading e-commerce company that adopted Copilot to accelerate the development of its web application. Facing tight deadlines and a growing backlog of features, the development team struggled to keep up with the demand for new code while maintaining high standards of quality. By integrating Copilot into their development workflow, the team was able to generate code snippets and templates quickly, reducing the time spent on repetitive coding tasks and freeing up valuable resources to focus on more complex challenges. As a result, the company was able to deliver new features to market faster and improve the overall user experience of its web application.

Another compelling case study comes from a financial services firm that implemented Copilot to enhance its code review process. With a large team of developers working on multiple projects simultaneously, the company faced challenges in ensuring code consistency and identifying potential issues early in the development lifecycle. By incorporating Copilot into their code review process, the team was able to leverage its suggestions to identify and fix coding errors, refactor code for better maintainability, and enforce coding standards across the organization. As a result, the company saw a significant improvement in code quality and a reduction in the number of bugs and issues reported in production.

In the healthcare industry, a leading provider of electronic medical records (EMR) software used Copilot to accelerate the development of new features and enhancements to its platform. With strict regulatory requirements and increasing demand for new functionality from healthcare providers, the development team needed a way to streamline their coding efforts without compromising on quality or security. By integrating Copilot into their development process, the team was able to leverage its AI-powered suggestions to generate code snippets for common tasks, such as data validation, error handling, and user interface design. This allowed them to reduce development time and effort while ensuring that the resulting code met industry standards and compliance requirements.

In the automotive industry, a manufacturer of autonomous vehicles utilized Copilot to optimize its software development process and accelerate innovation in vehicle technology. With the rapid advancement of autonomous driving technology and increasing competition in the market, the company needed a way to iterate quickly on new features and improve the performance and reliability of its software stack. By leveraging Copilot's code generation capabilities, the development team was able to prototype new algorithms and algorithms more efficiently, test different configurations, and optimize performance for real-world scenarios. This enabled the company to stay ahead of the competition and deliver cutting-edge autonomous driving solutions to its customers.

In summary, case studies of successful Copilot implementation in industry highlight the diverse applications and benefits of integrating this AI-powered tool into software development workflows. From accelerating development cycles and improving code quality to enhancing team collaboration and driving innovation, Copilot offers organizations a powerful solution for overcoming common challenges and achieving their goals in software development. By learning from these real-world examples and best practices, organizations can unlock the full potential of Copilot and harness its capabilities to drive success in their own projects and initiatives.

Real-world usage of Copilot has provided invaluable insights into the best practices and lessons learned by developers and organizations across various industries. These experiences offer practical guidance on how to effectively leverage Copilot's capabilities, optimize its integration into development workflows, and overcome common challenges encountered during usage.

One of the key lessons learned from real-world Copilot usage is the importance of understanding its strengths and limitations. While Copilot excels at generating code snippets and providing suggestions for common programming tasks, it's essential for developers to recognize that it's not a substitute for human expertise. Developers should approach Copilot as a tool to augment their own coding abilities rather than relying on it blindly. By combining Copilot's suggestions with their own knowledge and experience, developers can ensure the quality and integrity of the code they produce.

Another best practice that has emerged from real-world Copilot usage is the importance of providing context when requesting suggestions. Copilot's ability to generate relevant and accurate code depends heavily on the information provided by the developer about the task at hand. By providing clear and concise descriptions of the problem to be solved, along with any relevant code snippets or examples, developers can improve the accuracy and relevance of Copilot's suggestions. Additionally, providing context helps Copilot understand the developer's intent and generate more useful and meaningful code snippets.

Effective communication and collaboration among team members are also critical for successful Copilot usage. Teams that have adopted Copilot have found that regular communication and collaboration help ensure that everyone is on the same page and working towards common goals. By sharing knowledge, discussing coding challenges, and providing feedback on Copilot's suggestions, team members can leverage each other's expertise and make better use of Copilot's capabilities. Collaborative tools such as version control systems and code review platforms can further facilitate communication and collaboration among team members.

Real-world usage of Copilot has also highlighted the importance of continuous learning and adaptation. As developers gain experience with Copilot and become more familiar with its capabilities, they can refine their usage patterns and develop strategies for maximizing its effectiveness. Additionally, as Copilot evolves and improves over time, developers must stay informed about new features and updates and adapt their workflows accordingly. By embracing a mindset of continuous learning and adaptation, developers can stay ahead of the curve and ensure that they are making the most of Copilot's capabilities.

Furthermore, real-world usage of Copilot has underscored the importance of maintaining code quality and adhering to best practices. While Copilot can expedite the coding process and help developers overcome common programming challenges, it's essential to prioritize code quality and ensure that the resulting code is maintainable, scalable, and free of bugs and vulnerabilities. This requires developers to review and test Copilot-generated code thoroughly, adhere to coding standards and best practices, and incorporate feedback from code reviews and quality assurance processes.

Additionally, organizations that have adopted Copilot have emphasized the importance of establishing clear guidelines and policies for its usage. By defining roles and responsibilities, setting expectations for how Copilot should be used, and providing training and support to developers, organizations can ensure that Copilot is integrated into their development workflows effectively and responsibly. Clear guidelines can also help mitigate potential risks and ensure that Copilot is used in a way that aligns with organizational goals and objectives.

In summary, real-world Copilot usage has provided valuable insights into best practices and lessons learned for effectively leveraging this AI-powered tool in software development. By understanding its strengths and limitations, providing context when requesting suggestions, fostering communication and collaboration among team members, embracing continuous learning and adaptation, prioritizing code quality, and establishing clear guidelines for usage, developers and organizations can make the most of Copilot's capabilities and drive success in their development projects.

Chapter 10: The Future of AI in Development with Copilot

Emerging trends and innovations in AI development tools are reshaping the landscape of software development, offering developers powerful new capabilities and transforming the way they build applications. One of the most notable trends in recent years is the growing adoption of AI-powered tools and platforms that automate various aspects of the development process, from code generation to testing and deployment. These tools leverage machine learning algorithms to analyze code patterns, identify bugs and vulnerabilities, and provide intelligent suggestions and recommendations to developers. As a result, developers can write code faster, with fewer errors, and more efficiently than ever before.

One of the key innovations driving this trend is the development of AI-powered code generation tools, such as OpenAI's Codex and GitHub Copilot. These tools use natural language processing and machine learning techniques to understand the intent behind code snippets and generate corresponding code automatically. For example, developers can use Codex or Copilot to describe a programming task in plain English, and the tool will generate the code needed to accomplish that task. This dramatically speeds up the coding process, reduces the need for manual coding, and helps developers focus on higher-level aspects of software development.

Another emerging trend in AI development tools is the use of AI for code analysis and optimization. Tools like DeepCode and CodeGuru use machine learning algorithms to analyze code repositories, identify potential bugs and security vulnerabilities, and provide recommendations for improving code quality and performance. By leveraging AI-driven code analysis, developers can catch errors early in the development process, streamline code reviews, and ensure that their applications are more robust and secure.

Furthermore, AI-driven testing and debugging tools are becoming increasingly popular among developers. These tools use machine learning algorithms to automatically generate test cases, detect bugs, and identify areas of code that are prone to errors. For example, tools like Diffblue and Mabl use AI to generate test scripts based on code changes, execute tests automatically, and identify regression issues. By automating testing and debugging tasks, these tools help developers detect and fix bugs more quickly, leading to faster release cycles and more reliable software.

Additionally, AI-powered tools are revolutionizing the field of natural language processing (NLP) and making it easier for developers to build applications that understand and generate human language. Technologies like GPT (Generative Pre-trained Transformer) have enabled developers to create chatbots, virtual assistants, and other NLP-driven applications with unprecedented levels of accuracy and fluency. These tools can understand context, generate coherent responses, and even perform tasks such as summarizing documents or translating text between languages.

Another emerging trend in AI development tools is the use of AI for data analysis and machine learning. Tools like TensorFlow and PyTorch provide powerful frameworks for building and training machine learning models, while platforms like DataRobot and H2O.ai offer automated machine learning solutions that enable developers to build predictive models with minimal manual intervention. By democratizing access to machine learning and data analysis capabilities, these tools are enabling developers to build intelligent applications that can analyze data, make predictions, and learn from experience.

Moreover, AI-driven development environments are becoming increasingly popular among developers, offering intelligent features and workflows that streamline the development process. For example, Microsoft's Visual Studio IntelliCode uses machine learning to provide intelligent code completion suggestions, while JetBrains' IntelliJ IDEA offers AI-powered code inspections and refactoring tools. These tools help developers write cleaner, more efficient code, reduce errors, and improve productivity.

Furthermore, the integration of AI into version control systems and collaborative development platforms is another emerging trend in AI development tools. Platforms like GitHub and GitLab are incorporating AI-driven features such as code review assistance, automated issue triaging, and intelligent code search. These features help developers collaborate more effectively, share knowledge, and maintain code quality across distributed teams.

In summary, emerging trends and innovations in AI development tools are transforming the way software is built, enabling developers to write code faster, more efficiently, and with fewer errors. By leveraging AI-powered code generation, analysis, testing, and debugging tools, developers can build more reliable, secure, and intelligent applications that meet the demands of today's rapidly evolving technology landscape. As AI continues to advance, we can expect to see even more exciting developments in AI development tools in the years to come.

Speculating on the evolution of Copilot and its impact on software development opens up a realm of possibilities for the future of coding. Since its introduction, Copilot has already made significant waves in the developer community, showcasing the potential of AI to augment the coding process. However, its journey is far from over, and there are numerous directions in which it could evolve to further revolutionize software development.

One potential avenue for Copilot's evolution is the refinement and expansion of its code generation capabilities. As it continues to learn from vast amounts of code and developer interactions, Copilot could become even more adept at understanding and anticipating developer intent. This could lead to more accurate and contextually relevant code suggestions, further reducing the need for manual coding and enabling developers to focus on higher-level aspects of software design and architecture.

Furthermore, Copilot could evolve to become more deeply integrated into development workflows and tools. For example, it could seamlessly integrate with popular IDEs (Integrated Development Environments) such as Visual Studio Code or IntelliJ IDEA, providing real-time code suggestions and assistance as developers write code. Additionally, Copilot could be integrated with version control systems like Git, enabling it to learn from and contribute to shared code repositories, facilitating collaboration and code reuse across teams.

Another area of evolution for Copilot is in the realm of software testing and debugging. Currently, Copilot primarily focuses on code generation, but it could potentially expand its capabilities to assist with writing unit tests, generating test data, and even automatically detecting and fixing bugs. By leveraging its understanding of code patterns and best practices, Copilot could help developers write more robust and reliable software, leading to fewer defects and faster release cycles.

Moreover, Copilot could evolve to provide support for a wider range of programming languages, frameworks, and libraries. While it currently supports several popular languages such as Python, JavaScript, and C++, expanding its language support would make it accessible to an even broader audience of developers working in different tech stacks. This could include support for emerging languages and technologies, as well as specialized domains such as machine learning or blockchain development.

In addition to expanding its technical capabilities, Copilot could also evolve to address broader challenges in software development, such as accessibility and inclusivity. For example, it could provide assistance for writing more accessible code that complies with accessibility standards and guidelines. It could also offer support for developers with disabilities, such as by providing voice-activated commands or integrating with screen readers.

Furthermore, Copilot could evolve to become more customizable and adaptable to individual developer preferences and workflows. For example, developers could fine-tune its suggestions based on coding style preferences, project-specific conventions, or domain-specific requirements. Additionally, Copilot could offer more granular control over its behavior, allowing developers to adjust the level of assistance provided or customize the types of suggestions it offers.

Another intriguing possibility for Copilot's evolution is the incorporation of collaborative features that enable real-time pair programming and code reviews. By facilitating synchronous collaboration between developers, Copilot could help teams work more efficiently and effectively, fostering knowledge sharing and collective problem-solving. This could include features such as shared code editing sessions, integrated video conferencing, and collaborative commenting and annotation tools.

Furthermore, Copilot could evolve to incorporate more advanced AI techniques such as reinforcement learning or natural language understanding. This could enable it to better understand and respond to developer queries and commands, as well as adapt its behavior based on feedback and interactions. For example, it could learn from how developers respond to its suggestions and adjust its recommendations accordingly to better align with their preferences and coding style.

Overall, the evolution of Copilot holds tremendous potential to reshape the landscape of software development in the years to come. By continuing to innovate and expand its capabilities, Copilot could empower developers to build better software faster, while also fostering a more collaborative and inclusive development environment. As AI technology continues to advance, the possibilities for Copilot's evolution are virtually limitless, and its impact on software development is likely to be profound and far-reaching.

Conclusion

In this comprehensive book bundle, "GitHub Copilot for Developers: Smart Coding with AI Pair Programmer," readers have been provided with a thorough exploration of the capabilities and potential of AI-assisted programming, specifically focusing on GitHub Copilot. Across four distinct volumes, developers have embarked on a journey from introductory concepts to advanced techniques, equipping themselves with the knowledge and skills needed to leverage Copilot effectively in their development workflows.

Book 1, "GitHub Copilot Companion: An Introduction to AI-Assisted Programming," served as the gateway to understanding the fundamentals of Copilot's AI-powered code generation capabilities. Through practical examples and hands-on exercises, readers gained insight into how Copilot can augment their coding experience, providing contextually relevant suggestions and speeding up development cycles.

In Book 2, "Mastering AI Pair Programming: Advanced Techniques for Developers," readers delved deeper into the intricacies of AI pair programming, exploring advanced techniques and strategies for maximizing productivity and efficiency. By mastering Copilot's features and integrating them seamlessly into their workflow, developers learned how to tackle complex coding challenges with confidence and precision.

Book 3, "Efficient Coding with GitHub Copilot: Strategies for Intermediate Developers," catered to the needs of intermediate developers seeking to enhance their coding proficiency and streamline their development processes. Through a series of best practices and optimization strategies, readers learned how to leverage Copilot's capabilities to write cleaner, more maintainable code and accelerate their software development efforts.

Finally, in Book 4, "Expert Insights: Leveraging GitHub Copilot for Complex Development Tasks," readers gained access to expert insights and real-world use cases showcasing the full potential of Copilot in addressing complex development tasks. From refactoring legacy codebases to scaling Copilot usage for large-scale projects, developers learned how to harness Copilot's AI capabilities to overcome challenges and drive innovation in their projects.

As this book bundle comes to a close, readers are equipped with the knowledge, skills, and strategies needed to harness the power of GitHub Copilot effectively in their development endeavors. Whether they are beginners exploring the possibilities of AI-assisted programming or seasoned professionals seeking to optimize their workflows, this bundle serves as a comprehensive guide to unlocking the full potential of Copilot for developers of all levels. With AI as their trusted pair programmer, developers can embark on their coding journey with confidence, efficiency, and creativity, paving the way for a future of smarter, more collaborative software development.

www.ingramcontent.com/pod-product-compliance
Lightning Source LLC
Chambersburg PA
CBHW071234050326
40690CB00011B/2118

* 9 7 8 1 8 3 9 3 8 7 5 5 5 *